The Next Economic Disaster

Why It's Coming and How to Avoid It

Richard Vague

PENN

UNIVERSITY OF PENNSYLVANIA PRESS

PHILADELPHIA

Published by
University of Pennsylvania Press
Philadelphia, Pennsylvania 19104-4112
www.upenn.edu/pennpress

Printed in the United States of America

A Cataloging-in-Publication Record is
available from the Library of Congress

Jacket design by John Hubbard

ISBN 978-0-8122-4704-6
eISBN 978-0-8122-9110-0

Contents

Appendices can be found online at
http://www.debt-economics.org/appendix.

The US economy is elbowing its way to recovery. In fact, booms have returned to some pockets of the economy. Unemployment is still painfully high but is coming down. The stock market is at historic highs. The rest of the world is struggling back as well.

There is one statistic that could return the global economy to the terrible old days of 2007–2008. It is one I learned about during my thirty years in banking, much of that time spent as cofounder, president, and then CEO of one of the nation's largest consumer lenders. Although my bank did not make mortgage loans, from my ringside seat to the lending industry, I saw the massive increase in mortgage loans starting in the early 2000s that helped make me an expert on an underrecognized yet critical economic indicator: private debt. That might sound esoteric, but it's crucially important. This one element in the economy is responsible for the financial crisis of 2008 and will precipitate the next one if it goes unheeded.

The idea that private debt can accumulate to the point that it is harmful comes from the very beginnings of civilization. On some occasions when debt had increased to high levels, rulers in places like ancient Egypt, Babylon, and Israel canceled debts of the people and gave them a clean slate.

Closer to home, between 2001 and 2004, US household mortgage debt increased a mind-boggling 48 percent. I worried that the inevitable bad loans from this mortgage tsunami could engulf our business as well. So I asked industry economists about it, only to hear that since the value of consumer homes and stock holdings had increased more than mortgage loans, there was no cause to worry. As a lender, I knew that even if that were true, consumers would have to sell assets to pay back their now significantly higher levels of debt, and that meant our industry was in for terrible problems. It did not matter that I was not in that particular business. Just as a rising tide lifts all boats, a tsunami overwhelms everyone. We were all going down with the ship.

And so we did. By 2007, this same mortgage debt had increased by an unthinkable 99 percent in just six years, and the financial industry was soon overwhelmed by the greatest crisis since the Great Depression. Some perished. It is a miracle that anyone survived.

There were many arguments over who and what were to blame. As it became clear to me that the frenetic growth of private loans was the culprit, I wondered whether rapid loan growth was the cause of other epochal crises—such as the Great Depression and the Japan Banking Crisis of 1991. And if so, was private debt the only cause, or were there other factors? If I answered those questions, could we realistically predict and prevent future crises?

Before I could begin to look for answers, the debate was hijacked by loud voices invested in moving the debate over to government debt and a very different and rancorous discussion of "austerity vs. stimulus." Despite the noise, I conducted my own investigation of these issues, hiring a team of economists as part of the effort. When we started to dig in, we found that data and analysis of private debt were not as readily available as we would have thought, particularly outside the United States, so we set out to gather and analyze that data ourselves.

The results were eye-opening.

In fact, they were so unexpected that I took the further step of visiting with dozens (and dozens) of different economists with a broad spectrum of viewpoints to get their sense of my findings. The reactions ranged from rejection to enthusiasm, but they were always instructive. I retained a second group of economists to poke holes in the findings of the first team. I listened carefully. This book is the result of all that work. It tells the story of past crises (as opposed to mere recessions), a prediction of a looming crisis we may collectively face, and an analysis of the paradox of debt itself.

Lurking underneath is a deeper concern about the long-term trend line of private debt in our nation and the world. Private debt has grown faster than income and GDP (gross domestic product, a measure of the size of a country's economy) for a very long time—going back two hundred years, in fact. A high level of private debt makes an economy more vulnerable to crises and impedes stronger growth. So continuing this trend will assuredly bring escalating problems. Whatever else it is, this book is my modest contribution to a debate about the central role of private debt in economic trends and the wisdom of changing the global course from its current, perilous path.

Chapter 1

Boom and Crisis

Most mainstream economists failed to predict the greatest economic crisis[1] of our lifetime: the global financial crisis of 2007–2008.[2] In fact, many viewed the economy as healthy or robust even as the crisis loomed. Yet their theories remain largely unchanged, leaving off-target their prescriptions to mend the still-damaged global economy and to reduce continued economic stress.

In the aftermath of this crisis, most of the debate has been on the subject of government debt—on "austerity vs. stimulus." One side blames government debt for impeding economic growth and thus prescribes a reduction in government spending called "austerity," while the other side calls for more government deficit spending as the necessary "stimulus" for strong economic growth.

Both sides miss a much more central point.

The primary issue is not public debt but private debt. It was the runaway growth of private debt—the total of business and household debt—coupled with a high overall level of private debt that led to the crisis of 2008. And even today, after modest deleveraging, the level of private debt remains high and impedes stronger economic growth.

Rapid private debt growth also fueled what were viewed as triumphs in their day—the Roaring Twenties, the Japanese "economic miracle" of the '80s, and the Asian boom of the '90s—but each of these were debt-fueled binges that brought these economies to the brink of economic ruin.

Those crises are the best known, but almost all crises in major countries have been caused by rapid private debt growth coupled with high overall levels of private debt. The reverse is true as well; almost all instances of rapid debt growth coupled with high overall levels of private debt have led to crises.

There are two claims you can count on: Booms come from rapid loan growth. And crises come from booms.

Alan Greenspan, who was chairman of the Federal Reserve until 2006 and who presided over much of the runaway increase in mortgage loans that was central to the 2008 crisis, wrote recently in reference to this crisis that "financial bubbles occur from time to time, and usually with little or no forewarning."[3]

Alan Greenspan is wrong.

It was neither a "black swan event" nor a crisis in confidence. There was plenty of forewarning—in fact years' worth. This crisis was predictable, and major financial crises of this type can be seen—and prevented—well in advance.

Beyond the issue of rapid short-term loan growth, the United States has been on a long-term and continual path of increasing private debt to GDP. It is astonishing what's happened: over the past seventy years, the level of private debt to income and GDP—in the United States and across the entire globe—has climbed steeply higher. In the United States, it has almost tripled from 55 percent in 1950 to 156 percent today. What is equally astonishing is how little attention it has received.

While runaway loan growth was the cause of the crisis, loan growth at a more moderate level is a favorable driver of economic growth. This is the seeming paradox that is one of the subjects of this book.

(Note: I will use the terms *economic growth* and *GDP growth* interchangeably in this book—GDP growth is simply the sum of private, business, and government spending plus net exports. And income closely mirrors GDP, so whenever I mention GDP growth, it encompasses income growth too.)

When debt growth is too rapid, it brings economic calamity, especially if coupled with private debt levels that are already too high, since high private debt levels make businesses and consumers more vulnerable to economic distress.

In this book, I will argue that for large economies, private loan to a GDP growth of roughly 18 percent or more in five years is the level where that growth is excessive. (I'll discuss the few exceptions later.) On top of this, apart from any crisis, the accumulation of higher levels of private debt over decades impedes stronger growth. Money that would otherwise be spent on things such as business investment, cars, homes, and vacations is increasingly diverted to making payments on that rising level of debt— especially among middle- and lower-income groups that compose most of our population and whose spending is necessary to drive economic growth. Debt, once accumulated, constrains demand. And debt growth here and abroad over any sustained period always exceeds the income and economic growth it helps create, a troubling phenomenon intrinsic to the system.

Economists refer to the rise in private debt to GDP as part of "financial deepening," and many view it as a hallmark of economic growth. But just as it is for individuals and businesses, so it is for the economy as a whole—some private debt can be good, but too much is not.

Both the rapid growth of private debt and high absolute levels of private debt get scant attention. Most attention has instead gone to public debt. No one has proposed a systemic way to address this private debt problem.

I hope to help correct that deficit. A key objective of this book is to put the spotlight on private debt, to examine its central place in the economy, and to propose ways to address it so we don't end up repeating the crisis of 2008.

There is a reason that economists have focused on public debt more than private debt. Public debt seems like much more of a public responsibility—it is "we the people's" job to manage public debt. Private debt seems off-limits, more like meddling in the private sector and free enterprise with a whiff of Big Brother. Private loan growth—especially in housing and business—is viewed as always being good for us, so "hands off."

But this is utterly false. GDP growth is influenced by private debt growth as much as, or more than, any other factor. Runaway growth in private debt, especially when combined with high existing levels of that debt, is what has caused most major economic crises of the last century. That makes it a very public issue. Public policy profoundly influences private loan growth, especially through direct and indirect capital requirements imposed on lenders.

There is one more reason private debt is more susceptible to crisis than public debt. Governments with their own currency can, within reason, print money or raise taxes. Private businesses or individuals cannot. Businesses and households more quickly reach the limits of solvency because they must generate income to service and repay the debts.

Many authors have done solid work in portraying the role of private debt in crises—Irving Fisher, Hyman Minsky, Alan Taylor, and Morris Shularick, among others. My principal addition to their work is the specific algorithm for predicting and preventing future crises featured in this book. Of recent note is the helpful work of Atif Mian and Amir Sufi in *House of Debt*. They argue, as I do, that household mortgage debt was the 2008 crisis culprit and that restructuring mortgage debt is a productive way to inspire growth. Further, they demonstrate that debt drives asset values rather than the other way around, and that the problematic mortgage debt burden that led to the Great Recession fell disproportionately on middle- and lower-income groups. To their work, I add the algorithm mentioned previously for predicting crises, argue that business debt growth is often equally culpable to household debt in causing crises, extend this analysis to all major economies, and emphasize capital requirements as the primary means for preventing future crises.

The Centrality of Private Debt

The financial crisis of 2008—which brought on the Great Recession—arrived in an avalanche of mortgage loans. Builders built more homes than were needed, lenders made mortgage loans that borrowers couldn't repay, and this orgy of lending itself pushed the prices of homes above sustainable levels, compounding the problem when values collapsed from those artificial highs to levels below loan amounts.

This high mortgage loan growth was part of an overall runaway growth in private debt, and it was private debt growth—not growth in government debt, a lack of consumer or business confidence, or any of the myriad other explanations—that was the immediate cause of the 2008 crisis. US mortgage debt grew from $5.3 trillion in 2001 to $10.6 trillion in 2007, an astonishing doubling in six years. This contributed to high absolute levels of private debt to GDP, a level that reached 173 percent in 2008. In larger, more developed economies, when high growth in private debt is coupled with high absolute levels of private debt, it has almost always led to calamity. Since this buildup of excessive private debt occurred over several years, it should have made the prediction of the crisis and its prevention both possible and straightforward.

But it wasn't just mortgage loans. Business debt to GDP picked up markedly starting in 2006, and overall private debt increased at a pace rarely seen during the last century in the United States—an increase of 20 percent to GDP in the five years leading up to the crisis. (See Chart 1.)

By contrast, in 2007, the federal government debt to GDP was slightly lower than it had been ten years before and didn't accelerate until after the crisis. Benign growth in government debt is typical of the period preceding most significant financial crises.

As Chart 2 shows, from the sheer dollar amounts involved, it should be no surprise that private debt would be a primary driver of the economy. This chart shows the

Chart 1: US Mortgage and Private Debt to GDP Growth

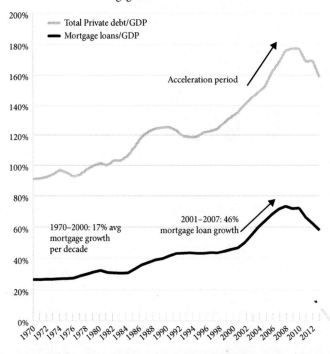

Sources: GDP data from Bureau of Economic Analysis; private debt and mortgage loans data from Federal Reserve.

increase in key categories from 1997 to 2007—the decade preceding the crisis:

From 1997 to 2007, lenders flooded the US economy with $14.4 trillion in net new private loans. Federal debt increased by a significantly smaller amount—$3.6 trillion—during that same period. An increase in bank loans represents the entry of additional money into the economy. For all the talk of the US government and the Federal Reserve Bank "printing money," it is private lending that creates the most new money entering the

Chart 2: Key Item Comparison, 1997–2007

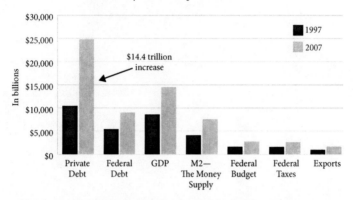

Sources: GDP and exports data from Bureau of Economic Analysis; private debt and M2 data from Federal Reserve; federal budget and federal taxes data from CBO; federal debt data from treasurydirect.gov.

economy. The primary constraint on that new money flooding the economy is the capital requirements imposed on those lenders. Anyone who has been granted a loan and had the proceeds of that loan deposited into his or her account has just witnessed the deposit of newly created money into the system. The idea that savings and deposit growth must precede loan growth and thus leads to loan growth is misguided. Instead, loans create money and are thus a part of what creates deposits.

For this reason, total loans are a more accurate gauge of the amount of money in an economy than the "money supply" (the sum of deposits and currency), which is in large part a by-product of that lending.

The impact of private loans in this period far exceeds the impact of any other category. For example, a 10 percent reduction in taxes for each of these ten years would have brought no more than a $2.5 trillion increase in spending by the private sector, an amount dwarfed by the

$14.4 trillion in new private sector spending enabled by this increase in private loans.

As Chart 3 shows, private debt growth is much more closely tied to GDP growth than public debt growth, more evidence that when it comes to debt, it's private, not public, debt that's the primary driver of GDP growth. (And when private debt growth sharply exceeds GDP growth, which economists call increased "credit intensity," it is evidence that too many bad loans are being made. See similar charts for Japan and China in Appendix A. All appendices can be found online at http://www.debt-economics.org/appendix.) Further, as noted by Dr. Steve Keen, private debt growth is also tightly correlated to employment growth (see Appendix B).

Many formally trained economists—as opposed to investment and business practitioners—have not focused on the question of the relationship between debt and

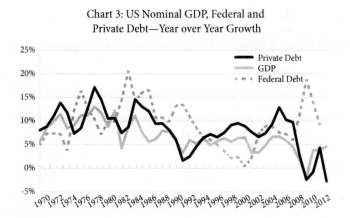

Chart 3: US Nominal GDP, Federal and
Private Debt—Year over Year Growth

Sources: GDP data from Bureau of Economic Analysis; federal debt data from treasurydirect.gov; private debt data from Federal Reserve.

growth but instead mainly concern themselves with savings and investment and productivity growth. Productivity gains are, of course, a fundamental driver of growth. But the thesis of this book is that private debt is also a primary driver of growth, especially since it is one of the primary determinants of investment and helps create deposits. Leverage can expand the availability of liquid capital. As leverage increases, so does the amount available to finance business expansion and consumer and household purchases.

Private debt growth is integral to GDP growth. But very rapid growth in private debt often leads to calamity because it is evidence that lenders have lent too much and those loans are leading to the construction or production of too much of *something*, such as housing. I consider this the "excess credit point." Our view is that roughly 18 percent growth in private debt to GDP growth over five years serves as the benchmark for when lending is excessive. This is especially true when that level of growth persists for several years and is coupled with 150 percent or more in absolute private debt to GDP. It signals that debt has fueled an increase in the supply of that something (e.g., housing) at a rate faster than sustainable demand. That something can vary from crisis to crisis. In the lead-up to the 2008 crisis, it was largely houses, but in other crises, it has been everything from stocks to skyscrapers.

When I say private debt to GDP grew 18 percent in five years, it means that the private debt to GDP ratio in, for example, 1997, was 18 percent greater than the private debt to GDP ratio in 1992. And if I say that five-year private debt to GDP growth was over 18 percent for two years in a row, it means that, for example, the 1997 ratio was over 18 percent higher than in 1992, and the 1998 ratio was over 18 percent higher than in 1993. I will refer to these five-year growth rates throughout the book.

In fact, whenever you see very rapid loan growth, it is likely that the following three things have happened: First, lenders have lent amounts that will not be fully repaid and financed the building of too much of something. Second, prices have increased well above the trend for those asset categories where the lending has been concentrated (e.g., housing) primarily as a result of that lending, giving both lenders and borrowers a false sense of confidence. And third, because so many bad loans have been made, lenders will incur large losses and require assistance—the very definition of a financial crisis.

A rise in asset values is regularly present in these overlending situations, but it is a dangerously circular phenomenon, because it is the overlending itself that is often the primary driver of this increase. *Lending policy itself is a primary driver of values.* If everything else is the same and lenders change from requiring a 25 percent down payment on houses to a 10 percent down payment, housing prices will increase—because there will now be more eligible buyers lining up at open houses on Sunday. This loan-policy-driven increase in prices generally encourages even more building and buying because the upward price movement makes housing seem like an even better investment.

Here is one other example: if lenders generally make loans to those wanting to buy a small business at three times the pretax earnings of those businesses, then those businesses will likely be valued at not much higher than three times pretax earnings. However, if most lenders then change their policies to lend at five times pretax earnings, small business values will then tend to increase to an amount of roughly five times their pretax earnings—even if there is no fundamental change in the performance of those businesses. It's circular.[4]

It takes only changes in lending policy to change values, but it takes actual income to sustain those values. If lending policy pushes values beyond what can be supported by the borrowers' incomes—as was the case with much of the mortgage lending in the years before the 2008 crisis—it creates unsustainable values and a false sense of wealth and confidence. Lenders pull back, and booming markets like Las Vegas and Phoenix are suddenly engulfed by "For Sale" signs.

Tripwire: Rapid Private Debt Growth

The press trumpets increases in business loans as a sign that better days are ahead. The housing market is viewed as a key driver of the overall economy, so increases in mortgage loans—which are roughly 70 percent of all consumer loans—are applauded as a sign of the resurgence of this market. Only increases in student loans (and to a lesser extent, credit card loans) are viewed with concern and not because of their impact on the economy, but because of a protective posture toward consumers.

Growth in private loans is generally a positive, but it is a central thesis of this book that such growth can become too high. If credit standards are relaxed and the result is that loans grow too rapidly and too much gets built or produced, that spells trouble.

While US private debt to GDP growth is currently flat, as shown in Charts 4a and 4b (which I refer to as the "debt snapshot"[5]), the crisis of 2008 came after the point where private loans to GDP had grown 20 percent in five years and total private loans to GDP exceeded 170 percent. (Debt snapshots for all the crises discussed in this book can be found in Appendix C.)

I wondered whether this was also true for the crash of 1929, a crisis for which an endless variety of explanations have been offered. When we reviewed the data, just as in the period before the Great Recession, we saw a pronounced acceleration of lending in the mid- to late 1920s. By 1928, private loans to GDP had increased almost 20 percent, and private debt to GDP reached a towering 161 percent (see Charts 5a and 5b). In fact, this was the first peacetime moment in US economic history when these two "twin peaks" of debt were reached simultaneously, and it was perhaps a time of far less sophistication and resilience in financial markets. Lending in the 1920s was directed more toward business borrowers than was true in the 2008 crisis.

Chart 4a: Crisis of 2007–2008, US 1990–2012
Nominal GDP, Federal and Private Debt

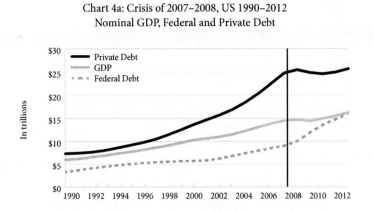

Sources: GDP data from Bureau of Economic Analysis; private debt data from Federal Reserve; federal debt data from treasurydirect.gov.

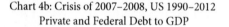

Chart 4b: Crisis of 2007–2008, US 1990–2012
Private and Federal Debt to GDP

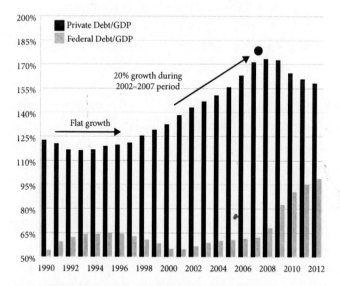

Sources: GDP data from Bureau of Economic Analysis; private debt data from Federeal Reserve; federal debt data from treasurydirect.gov.

In the 1920s, loans poured out to finance skyscrapers, business acquisitions, cars, homes, radios, and much more. Whatever other causes might have contributed to the crash of 1929 and the Great Depression, the rapid run-up in debt was central to the story.

Given the centrality of increased private debt to both the 1929 and 2008 calamities, we looked at the two other largest crises of the last generation to see if private debt played a part there as well: Japan's crisis of 1991, which followed its "economic miracle" of the 1980s, and the Asian crisis of 1997, which followed the "Asian economic miracle" of the 1990s. As shown in Charts 6a and 6b, in the period from 1985 to 1990, Japan's private debt to GDP

The Next Economic Disaster

Chart 5a: The Great Depression, US 1919–1939
Nominal GDP, Federal and Private Debt

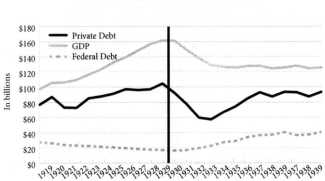

Sources: GDP (1929–1939) data from Bureau of Economic Analysis; all private debt data and GDP (1919–1928) data from Bureau of Economic Analysis, Survey of Current Business, October 1950; federal debt data from treasurydirect.gov.

Chart 5b: The Great Depression,
US 1919–1939 Private Debt to GDP

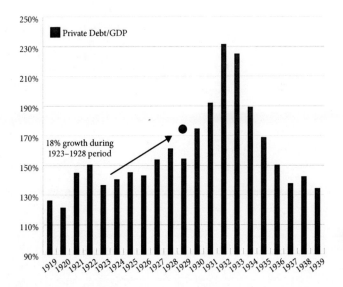

Sources: GDP (1929–1939) data from Bureau of Economic Analysis; all private debt data and GDP (1919–1928) data from Bureau of Economic Analysis, Survey of Current Business, October 1950.

increased by 28 percent and reached 213 percent of GDP. And in the five-year run-up to the Asian crisis of 1997, private loans to GDP for South Korea and Indonesia grew 29 percent and 43 percent, respectively, and in South Korea, private debt to GDP reached 170 percent.

Runaway lending created the Japanese and Asian economic miracles, but those miracles brought crisis.

Though less pronounced, even the Reagan revolution of the 1980s was in part the result of a simultaneous debt surge in both private and public debt that by 1987 had resulted in 19 percent private debt to GDP growth and 41 percent government debt to GDP growth in five years. (See Appendix C.) This followed a thirty-year period ending in 1980 in which, importantly, a long decline in government debt to GDP and increases in private debt to GDP had largely offset each other. As we would expect from our private debt hypothesis, this Reagan-era surge

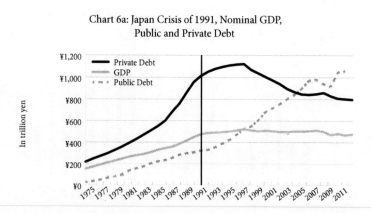

Chart 6a: Japan Crisis of 1991, Nominal GDP,
Public and Private Debt

Sources: GDP data from the United Nations; private debt data from BIS, "Long Series on Credit to Private Non-Financial Sectors"; public debt data from Reinhart & Rogoff.

Chart 6b: Japan Crisis of 1991,
Private and Public Debt to GDP

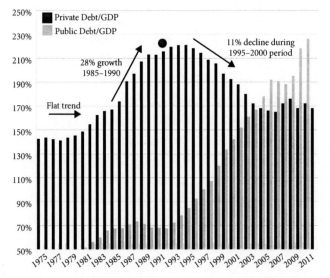

Sources: GDP data from United Nations; private debt data from BIS, "Long Series on Credit to Private Non-Financial Sectors" (ratios are author's calculations); public debt data from Reinhart & Rogoff.

in debt brought the crash of October 1987 and the savings and loan (S&L) crisis of the late 1980s and early 1990s.

Government debt to GDP was relatively benign before the crash of 1929, the US crisis of 2008, and both the Asian crisis of 1997 and the Japan crisis of 1991. In the United States, even with its Middle Eastern wars and a major increase in social program expenditures, federal debt to GDP was no higher in 2007 than it had been a decade before. The five-year increases in government debt to GDP in Japan in 1991 and South Korea in 1997 were both near zero.

In fact, the government debt to GDP ratio sometimes improves in the "runaway lending" period and becomes something of a contraindicator. In Spain, before its recent crisis, government debt to GDP declined by 16 percentage points. The credit boom brings increased income to businesses and consumers, and one result is more tax revenues for the government. Most businesses and consumers feel good, even euphoric, about their financial situation during this runaway lending period. And governments start believing they have found the recipe for economic success, such that the talk is often of economic miracles. But it shouldn't be, because the other economic shoe is now dangling and threatening to drop.

From our analysis of these crises, our hypothesis is that for major economies, growth in private debt to GDP of roughly 18 percent in five years combined with an overall private debt to GDP ratio of 150 percent or more means that a crisis is likely.

In the United Kingdom, the 2008 crisis came after it had reached 24 percent private credit to GDP growth in five years and 208 percent total private debt to GDP. Judged by the standard of private debt that we are using, the United Kingdom reached worse conditions than the United States. (See Charts 7a and 7b.)

The eurozone—eighteen European Union member states that have adopted the euro (€) as their common currency—has a combined current GDP of $13.1 trillion. However, four countries alone—Germany, France, Spain, and Italy—compose 70 percent of eurozone GDP. Study those four countries, and you have a good sense of the whole.

Spain's recent crisis came when it had reached private debt to GDP growth of 49 percent in five years and total private debt to GDP of 220 percent; France had reached 21 percent and 150 percent; and Italy had reached

Chart 7a: UK 2007–2008 Crisis, Nominal GDP,
Public and Private Debt

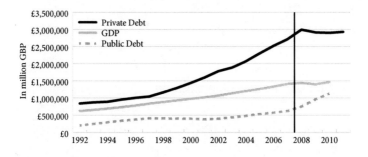

Sources: GDP data from United Nations; private debt data from BIS, "Long Series on Credit to Private Non-Financial Sectors"; public debt data from Reinhart & Rogoff.

Chart 7b: UK 2007–2008 Crisis,
Private and Public Debt to GDP

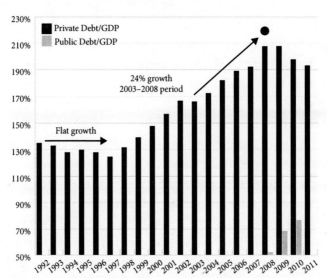

Sources: GDP data from United Nations; private debt data from BIS, "Long Series on Credit to Private Non-Financial Sectors" (ratios are author's calculations); public debt data from Reinhart & Rogoff.

33 percent and 118 percent. Of the four countries, Spain's lending trends were by far the most egregious (see Charts 8a and 8b). Notably, Germany only reached 122 percent and had a decline in private debt to GDP of 10 percent, but it had a crisis nonetheless because it is so inextricably intertwined with the other eurozone countries. Combined, the four countries had 19 percent growth in private debt to GDP and 144 percent total private debt. Germany is almost a special case because its export rate is so extraordinarily high relative to other countries. In 2012, Germany's exports to GDP were 52 percent, an enormous number compared to the United States' 13 percent, France's 27 percent, and Spain's 32 percent. Even China—which we think of as a massive exporter—only exports at a level of 27 percent of its GDP. (Therefore Germany is, in some respects, just as dependent on its neighbors as they are on it, though few frame it this way.) Germany's export dependence on other countries is so high that it is to some degree more useful to think of the eurozone as a single entity— economically at least—where a portion of the rise in private debt of other eurozone countries is to finance purchases from Germany.

As we have shown for other countries, government debt levels were benign and even improving in all these countries in large part because of the growth in private debt and the false prosperity that it brought.

Many of the countries at the periphery of the eurozone were and are in even worse shape. Note the debt snapshots of Greece, Portugal, and Ireland in Appendix C, with Greece's private debt to GDP growth of 58 percent in five years leading to its crisis. Portugal and Ireland's current private debt levels are 250+ percent and 300+

Chart 8a: Spain Nominal GDP, Private and Public Debt

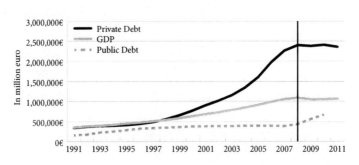

Sources: GDP data from United Nations; private debt data from BIS, "Long Series on Credit to Private Non-Financial Sectors"; public debt data from Reinhart & Rogoff.

Chart 8b: Spain Private and Public Debt to GDP

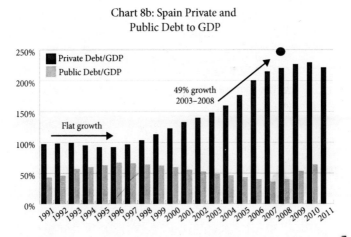

Sources: GDP data from United Nations; private debt data from BIS, "Long Series on Credit to Private Non-Financial Sectors" (ratios are author's calculations); public debt data from Reinhart & Rogoff.

percent, respectively, and hang like millstones around their economic necks.

Even though you would be hard-pressed to deduce this from press reports, the most critical current problem with the eurozone is the remaining high level of private debt. Of course, helping a given country in renewing maturing government debt or issuing new government debt—which is what most of the press reports are about—is important. But the persistent high level of private debt, not public debt, is what's crippling eurozone economies.

In Chapter 2, I underscore Europe's critical need to restructure its private debt.

The Long-Term Trend to Higher Debt

As we've seen, runaway private lending can lead to crisis. In addition to this, and in some part because of these episodes of runaway private lending, there has been a long-term trend toward higher and higher levels of private debt to GDP. This is not just a US trend; it is happening all over the globe. In China in particular, there has been startlingly high recent growth in private debt. Chart 9 illustrates this trend for the twenty largest economies of the world.

In 1950, US private debt stood at 55 percent of GDP. In 2014, it stood at 156 percent, almost tripling in two generations. After the 2008 crisis, the private sector deleveraged, with private debt to GDP declining from 173 percent to 156 percent. But that level is still 23 percentage points above the 133 percent level of private debt to GDP in 2000 and 56 percentage points above the 100 percent level of private debt to GDP in 1980.

Chart 9: Combined Twenty Largest World Economies,
Weighted Private and Public Debt as a Percentage of GDP

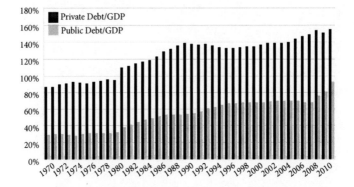

Sources: GDP data from United Nations; private debt data from Federal Reserve, CEIC, and BIS, "Long Series on Credit to Private Non-Financial Sectors" (ratios are author's calculations); public debt data from Reinhart & Rogoff and treasurydirect.gov.

This debt constrains demand.

An oft-heard refrain is "there is too little demand," especially from middle- and lower-income groups. To be sure, the continuing high level of unemployment is one reason for lower demand among these groups. But there should be no mystery regarding another key reason for this diminished demand—high levels of private debt. One crucial way to restore some portion of consumer and business demand is to reduce this debt. Lackluster demand is most often due not to the absence of confidence but to the burden of debt.

Private debt to GDP has been on a path of continual growth as businesses and consumers have become more leveraged. This increase has been especially pronounced during periods of runaway lending.

Lending booms generally result not just in a banking crisis with an adverse impact on GDP and employment; they also leave the economy with bad investments and higher levels of both private and public sector debt that can contribute disproportionately to an economy's buildup of debt over a longer period. It is as if each boom creates scar tissue that can't be fully removed and will create longer-term problems, especially if the debt is not properly restructured.

At any given time, some portion of private debt growth is inefficient (e.g., it finances projects that bring insufficient returns to repay the loan). The fact that some portion is inefficient is one reason private debt to GDP has been on a path of continual growth. In periods of

Chart 10: US Private and Federal Debt to GDP

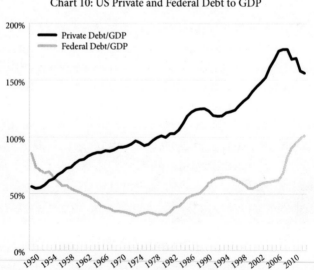

Sources: GDP data from Bureau of Economic Analysis; private debt data from Federal Reserve; federal debt data from treasurydirect.gov.

rapid debt growth, the portion that is inefficient rises sharply—though that inefficient debt contributes to a boom along the way. Looking at Chart 10, you can see this higher growth in the 1980s and 2000s. The more inefficient the use of private debt is, the more steep the upward slope of the line. The "horizontalness" or "verticalness" of the private debt to GDP ratio is itself an indicator of the efficiency and productiveness of the newly extended debt. The more flat the line—in other words, the less the ratio is increasing—the more efficiently that debt is being deployed into high-return uses. The more steep it is, the less efficiently it is being deployed. The same would hold true for total debt.

As shown in Chart 16, since the Industrial Revolution, we have been on a more than two-hundred-year march toward an ever-higher level of debt. And it is much more private debt than public debt. From a review of this long-term trend, it is clear that this is not a mere cycle, or supercycle, but instead a structural element of modern economies. Examining the data, modern economies simply don't grow over a long and sustained period unless private debt is growing at the same or a higher rate. Even if they could in theory grow without a commensurate private debt growth, they haven't in practice.

While it is outside the scope of this book to address growing income inequality and the role debt plays in that, it is important to note that this debt burden has caused a level of social stress in middle- and lower-income groups, domestically and globally, that remains high and troubling.

Critics make two arguments that seem to contradict a trend toward higher levels of private debt to GDP. The first is the assertion that businesses are "hoarding cash" just waiting for consumer confidence to return, or regulation to abate, in order to put that cash to work and jolt the economy forward. But in aggregate, there is little hoarding occurring. Business debt to total business assets (excluding goodwill and intangible assets) has been on a long-term increasing trend, and the total debt level of businesses far exceeds their liquid assets. While the liquid assets of businesses have increased relative to their short-term debt, in aggregate, the overall net debt position— total liabilities minus liquid assets—has been increasing. It is now 76 percent to GDP, down slightly from 80 percent in 2008, but at exactly the same level as a decade ago and up significantly from the 64 percent level in 1980.

The second argument is that some economists also believe the consumer has significantly deleveraged and is therefore in a good position to lead stronger economic growth. But consumer debt to GDP, though lower than in 2007, is still 12 percentage points higher than in 2000 and 64 percentage points higher than in 1980.

Oddly enough, the analysis of private debt is generally relegated to a peripheral place in economic analysis. Those who dismiss its importance—many of whom failed to see the impending 2008 crisis—make three arguments.

First, for the country as a whole, debt "nets to zero": For every borrower, there is a lender, and therefore the effect of any change on the country is neutral. This view ignores the disproportionate burden of this debt on middle- and lower-income groups, the very consumers that we depend on to power growth.

Second, analysts are comforted by the fact that interest rates are low, and the ratio of debt service to income is actually far below the crisis level of 2008. This view ignores the significant risk if interest rates do move higher. The US consumer "debt service ratio," the ratio of debt payments to income, has improved significantly in recent years. This is primarily because of the Federal Reserve's postcrisis bias toward "zero interest rates" to bolster the economy. It means that businesses and households pay less interest—the federal funds rate is down by a whopping 4 percentage points since the crisis—even if they have much higher debt than in the past. In this respect, it is giving false comfort, because that same business or household will have much higher payments when interest rates inevitably rise. In some respects, it is like the ultralow introductory rates provided by mortgage lenders that lured some borrowers into a false sense of comfort.

Third, analysts have discounted the importance of growth in private debt when they see it result in an increase in consumer or business net worth. In fact, in 2006–2007—the very period when we should have been most concerned by rising debt—many analysts were unconcerned by that rise because they could point to the fact that consumers' assets had increased more than their debt. Consumer net worth was at an all-time high.

This point is worth repeating: *In the period immediately before the 2008 crisis, consumer net worth was at a record high.* This was in large part because home values had increased. But when increasing debt is what leads to higher home or other asset values . . . beware! Values are ultimately constrained by income, and if values race ahead of the income required to support those values, they will come back to earth. Consumer net worth was also high because of a booming stock market, but it too was being fueled in part by record levels of margin debt and saw dramatic declines during the crisis. In aggregate, if debt is being created much faster than income—even if net worth is higher—a correction will occur.

It is private debt that matters most.

Testing the Thesis on All Major Economies

Some economists maintain that while private credit was the cause of the US crisis of 2008, there are many other types of financial crises with different causes.

I largely disagree.

In fact, simply stated, almost all financial crises in major countries have been caused by rapid private debt growth coupled with high overall levels of private debt. The reverse is true as well: Almost all instances of rapid debt growth coupled with high overall levels of private debt have led to crises.

I focus here on the twenty-two countries with a GDP of $500 billion or more. (See Appendix D; we exclude Iran because of no reliable data.) Together, they constitute 81 percent of world GDP. The United States and China together are a third of world GDP; including Japan, these three countries together are 40 percent of world GDP. The remaining one hundred and eighty countries beyond these twenty-two have far less than 1 percent of world GDP each. These small economies need to be analyzed separately from larger economies because even though private debt is still the predominant factor in their crises, they are more susceptible to other factors (e.g., industry concentrations, borrowings in a foreign currency, or the economic trends of a larger neighbor) than large countries. To put it bluntly, turmoil in the United States will have a big impact on Costa Rica, but turmoil in Costa Rica won't have much impact on the United States.

For these largest twenty-two countries, there have been a total of twenty-two crises where we have private debt available to analyze. Of these twenty-two, nineteen crises have been immediately preceded by growth of 18+ percent in private debt to GDP in five years (see Appendix E). Of the other three crises, two were in Germany and Switzerland in 2008, and while neither of those countries had high debt growth, they were intertwined with countries that did. The third was in India in 1993, which was a much smaller country economically at the time and susceptible to the additional factors affecting smaller countries mentioned previously.

So almost all these crises are preceded by 18+ percent growth in private debt to GDP in five years, but for our thesis to be correct, the reverse needs to be true as well: Instances where you find 18+ percent growth in private debt to GDP should result in a crisis. And that's largely been the case. As described presently, in almost all cases where you find the combination of 18+ percent growth in private debt in five years and a high overall level of private debt to GDP, the result has been a calamity.

Prior to 2000, for these largest countries, there were six times when countries have had both 18+ percent growth in private debt to GDP in five years and 150 percent absolute private debt to GDP. Four of these instances resulted in a crisis. The other two had a decline in real GDP. There were no "false positives"—instances where this rapid private lending growth occurred but were not followed by some type of economic reversal. There were no other crises for countries with 150 percent debt to GDP not preceded by rapid private debt growth.

A country-by-country schedule of this and the proceeding information can be found in Appendix E.

From 2000 onward, there were eleven times when countries have had both 18+ percent growth in private debt in a five-year span and 150 percent absolute private debt to GDP, and that lending boom has ended. Nine had either a crisis or a real GDP contraction. The remaining instances were Australia and South Korea, which in the late 2000s were carried along by the ongoing lending boom in their much larger neighbor China. The only crisis without a preceding boom was Switzerland in 2008, but that crisis resulted from its interconnectedness with countries that did in fact have a lending boom.

If you count the 2008 crisis as a single event rather than a separate event for each country, the results of this analysis are similar.

When combined, these two factors—18+ percent growth and a 150 percent absolute level of private debt—form a powerful predictor.

This formula is not hard and fast but indicative and useful.

Which brings us to China, the country that now has 54 percent growth in five-years in private debt to GDP and 182 percent overall private debt to GDP, and that I therefore deem to be "at risk." I discuss this more later in this chapter.

For countries with 18+ percent private debt to GDP growth in five years and a somewhat lower absolute level of private debt to GDP—a level between 100 percent and 149 percent—a lending boom is only slightly less predictive of a bad economic outcome. Of the thirteen times when countries at this level of private debt had a lending boom, ten had a crisis or a real GDP contraction.

There was only one crisis among this group not preceded by a credit boom, and that was Germany in 2008, where its banks lent in countries that did experience a boom, and that lending helped precipitate its crisis.

One caveat is that this 18+ percent only applies if total debt growth—public plus private—is at least 10 percent in the same period, because in some periods, private debt growth can be offset by public debt deleveraging. In these situations, the capacity being created by private lending is in part offset by contracting relative public spending. And this private debt growth brings higher GDP growth and accompanying tax revenues to aid in that public deleveraging. This was notably the case after World War II. In the United States, from 1955 to 1965, federal debt declined from 64 percent of GDP to 33 percent of GDP but was offset by very high private debt growth from 64 percent of GDP to 86 percent of GDP. (In fact, these "offsetting" trends—declining public debt to GDP offset by rising private debt to GDP—continued until the 1980s when they both began rising rapidly together.)

What is particularly noteworthy is the absence of other criteria to predict the risk of crisis in this group. I have long heard that such things as government debt, current account deficits, government deficits, and very low or declining real interest rates or currency trends are predictive of crises risk. In an extensive review of twenty other criteria for these countries, we saw significantly less or no power of these other criteria to predict crisis risk.

(See Appendix F.) For example, there are crises where real interest rates in the years immediately preceding the crisis are high and not descending. And there are periods where real interest rates are declining to very low levels that do not precipitate rapid loan growth and crisis.

Much has been made of the fact that the US crisis of 2008 was a result of mortgage loans, and as a result, some analysts have developed an extraordinary expertise in the details of mortgage lending. But there have been crises where mortgages have not played a big role but some other category of lending has. The key is that runaway lending in at least one category—be it commercial, industrial, real estate, or consumer—results in significant overcapacity and associated bad debt.

Much has also been made of the fact that in the US 2008 crisis, much lending occurred in the shadow banking sector, and there was also widespread use of instruments such as securitizations and credit default swaps. This allowed lenders to sidestep capital requirements and thus grow loans more rapidly than their capital would otherwise have allowed and helped separate the lenders from the risk associated with their lending decisions. Again, some analysts have developed enviable levels of expertise in these instruments as a result. Yet it is not the instrument of debt nor the type of lender but the debt itself that is the problem. Other crises have been precipitated by different types of instruments created to sidestep capital constraints or separate loan originators from risk. And future crises will likely be characterized by yet again different strategies or instruments to accomplish these things. And some crises have little in the way of such instruments.

That means that in some respects, you can put the instrument of debt and the type of lender aside and look simply at the aggregate growth of private loans from banks and all other types of lenders combined. That aggregate is a reliable top-down indicator of whether too much debt and too much capacity are being created. And the key to assessing capital adequacy is to look at those aggregates against aggregate "tangible" capital. The simple leverage ratio test advocated by former FDIC head Sheila Bair is a solid step in this direction.

My conclusion, for larger countries, is this: With a 100 percent private debt to GDP ratio and a credit boom, a calamity is probable. With a 150 percent private debt to GDP ratio and a credit boom, a calamity is almost certain.

After the lending boom starts, the calamity may be delayed, propped up for several years by continued lending. But almost inevitably, the crisis will come. After that, two things will have to happen for recovery to begin: First, overcapacity must be largely absorbed, and second, those lenders need to be recapitalized so that they can start lending again.

Some have said these crises come from a sudden lack of confidence on the part of consumers, businesses, or banks and further say that a return of good times depends primarily on a return of confidence. However, in 2007 and 2008, had consumers, businesses, and banks burst with confidence, it would not have changed the fact that far too many houses had been built and were sitting unsold and far too many unwise loans had been made that would not be fully repaid. Confidence disappeared only when consumers, lenders, and businesses discovered that too much lending and building had occurred, not the other way around. And confidence returns not when consumers, banks, and businesses "get a grip" on themselves, but instead it returns when enough of those homes have been sold, enough of those loans have been repaid, restructured, or otherwise rehabilitated, and enough lenders have been recapitalized and can refocus on growth.

We can now use the straightforward formula of the growth and level of private debt described here to predict calamity. It means crises are not ethereal things that arrive unannounced and are impossible to foresee, predict, and forestall. *The crisis of 2008 could have been seen—and curbed—many years in advance.* The lending boom was plainly evident by 2005 and had reached runaway proportions by 2007.

Stages of Crisis

From our study of these large economies, a rough pattern emerges for the stages leading to overlending and then to crisis. The pattern described presently is not meant to be precise; details vary from situation to situation. Rather it traces a typical course of events:

Stage I: Acceleration. Private lending to GDP accelerates after a somewhat benign period where lending growth to GDP is relatively flat. The acceleration happens for a variety of reasons—but it doesn't take much. Lenders make money by lending, so lending growth is pursued as the surest path to more income. Lenders might see an opportunity from external factors—a new product, technology, or commodity; relaxed scrutiny; a new way to sidestep regulatory capital requirements; a belief, founded or unfounded, that underlying asset valuations will rise—and they're off to the races.

Stage II: Mild Euphoria. Since lending creates new money and injects it into the economy, GDP growth responds favorably to loan growth; confidence mounts, and valuations rise in the sectors in which this lending is focused. Businesses hire and expand. This feeds on itself as confidence breeds overconfidence, which leads to . . .

Stage III: Rapid Lending Phase. If a little lending works, how about a lot of lending? Lending accelerates to runaway levels, which occur at about 18+ percent private debt to GDP growth in five years. Businesses (and consumers) consider this the new norm. They hire and expand further. Valuations continue to rise. The circularity spirals. Tax receipts improve, and governments get overconfident, often increasing their own spending as a result of the good news. An excess credit point has been reached. The market participants may not realize it yet, but when the excess credit point is reached, too much of something has already been built, and too many bad loans have already been made.

Stage IV: The Gap. This is the time between when the excess credit point is reached and the crisis starts. The boom may go on for a while, for many years in fact, as long as lenders keep lending. But it almost always ends badly. While our analysis shows a crisis can occur as soon as an 18+ percent level is reached, it still can go on for several years. (See Appendix G.) That's because the very act of more lending can put off a crisis, even if these loans are to projects that are no longer credit worthy—if ever they were. In real estate, for example, builders and developers can sometimes use new advances to make payments, or

China?

can remain in interest-only payment mode. The boom is self-sustaining for a while as the very act of lending itself brings ever more money into the economy. Stages III and IV are sometimes referred to as *booms* or *bubbles*.

GDP growth is in some part a measure of how much is being built or produced. Thus GDP is in some respects a measure of the capacity being created—as opposed to a measure of how much capacity is needed or can be absorbed. The common characteristic of all lending booms is that much more capacity is being created than is needed.

Once the party has started, it tends to go on for a while. But it won't go on forever. Once an excess credit point has been reached, problems are now present that only time and large amounts of capital can solve, even though a crisis may not yet have occurred. Some things only time can cure. If, for example, you have 500,000 extra homes on the market and organic demand (unaided by loose lending) is for only 100,000 houses a year, nothing but time can solve that issue. Monetary and fiscal policies are important here, but belief in their efficacy far exceeds reality. They can only soften the blow and help tide an economy over when an excess private credit point has been reached.

We might think that lenders would curtail lending before reaching this overcapacity point, but the long history of American and global banking provides ample evidence that they rarely do.

Stage V: Full-Blown Crisis. The profile of the collapse is never exactly the same, but generally, it goes like this: Companies' earnings begin to fall short, lenders find that an unavoidably large number of loans are in trouble, and certain markets that have shown a rapid rise, usually including the stock market, plunge. A market plunge doesn't result in a full-blown crisis if that rise has not been fueled by debt. Experience shows that it is too much private debt that leaves an economy exposed to this type of plunge.

Lenders realize they have reached this point when enough loans turn delinquent, even though this over-capacity point usually arrives before delinquency is a problem. The calamity generally doesn't truly begin until lenders turn the spigot off and begin to take actions to protect as much principal as possible, which often means discontinuing new loan advances or calling loans.

Triggering events like a bank failure or stock market crash are routinely and mistakenly viewed as causes of a crisis. But the overlending and overcapacity occurred prior to these events, and while the triggering event can factor into how little or much trauma is experienced, *it was the overlending that preceded it that was the cause.*

The result of the trigger is that the quality of banks and other lender's loans begins to be in doubt—enough so that the very safety of those institutions is in doubt. Once that occurs, depositors and lenders to those banks or other financial institutions begin withdrawing funds. There's a run on those institutions, which are then suddenly in jeopardy of failure.

"Contagion" begins to occur, spreading the crisis to other lenders in the same country and potentially to lenders in other countries. (For some countries, especially those with a high percentage of short-term government loans from foreign lenders, the contagion can also spread to those governments.) Contagion simply means that if lenders to financial institutions and depositors in those institutions have evidence that Bank A is troubled, they suspect that Bank B and Bank C are troubled as well, and they're not going to wait for proof one way or the other. They begin withdrawing their funds or elect not to renew loans to Bank B and Bank C, reasoning that it is better to be safe than sorry. So Bank B and Bank C are then forced to contract, and their own solvency is jeopardized.

Because of lenders' need to contract, they are forced to reduce or call the loans of many otherwise healthy individuals and businesses, harming many in the process. And the more widespread the run on lenders, the more those lenders have to contract, causing them to call still more loans and harm still more businesses and individuals in the process.

This all becomes self-reinforcing—the bigger the market collapse, the more doubt spreads and the more others sell. Since much stock purchasing is done on margin, falling stock prices themselves cause margin loans to be called, forcing even more stock sales and thus further declines in stock prices—which itself has an adverse impact on the economy, and so on.

In a crisis, lending losses are generally large enough that major lending institutions no longer have enough capital to operate and have to either shed loans, raise new capital, or seek the assistance of the government to continue operating.

Stage VI: Policy Response Begins. I discuss this more fully in Chapter 2.

Stage VII: The Aftermath. The aftermath is generally a prolonged period—no less than several years—characterized by a slowdown or decline in lending (after a period in which lending virtually stops), slumps in markets, declining or stagnant GDP, and high unemployment.

Chart 11a: China Nominal GDP,
Private and Public Debt

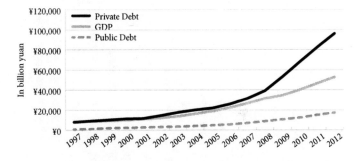

Sources: GDP data from United Nations; public debt data from People's Bank of China; private debt data for 1997–2012 from BIS, "Long Series on Credit to Private Non-Financial Sectors" and for 2008–2012 from CEIC.

China and Japan

Applying our private debt criteria to China, we can see that its economy is at risk of a major financial crisis in the near future, a significant concern because of its size and importance to the world economy. (See Charts 11a and 11b.)

The situation in China is alarming. The five-year growth in private credit to GDP is 54 percent. Its private debt to GDP ratio stands at 182 percent. (The numbers for China include "shadow lending" but are somewhat difficult to pin down, and I have seen numbers for the current level of private debt in China that range from 167 percent to 200+ percent, but in all cases, the recent five-year private debt to GDP growth trends are above 40 percent.)

I hold that once a country reaches an excess credit point, bad things will almost always happen. But I also maintain that excessive growth in lending can continue for a number of years prior to any crisis or adversity, and in China,

Chart 11b: China Private and Public Debt to GDP

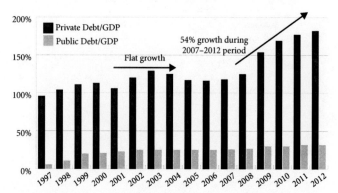

Sources: GDP data from United Nations; public debt data from People's Bank of China; private debt for 1997–2007 from BIS, "Long Series on Credit to Private Non-Financial Sectors" (ratios are author's calculations) and for 2008–2012 from CEIC.

it clearly has. However, the trends in China are changing for the worse. Real GDP growth has dropped from 14 percent in 2007 to 7.8 percent in 2012. China abounds in ghost cities—gleaming places that sit virtually empty because of a lack of demand—and equally concerning pockets of over-capacity in other sectors throughout its economy.

But China has ample capacity to prop up its economy for a time. It holds financial assets equal to 35 percent of its GDP, and with a central government debt of only 32 percent to GDP, it has plenty of borrowing capacity as well. Since it is a command economy, it has the straight-forward authority to manage its economy and direct its banks to keep increasing lending, or at least keep loans from declining despite the high level of problem loans. It can use regulatory prerogative to exercise forbearance on problem loans and capital requirements and use its financial assets and borrowing capacity to fortify these banks with additional capital.

"How much longer will China will be able to prop up its economy?" is perhaps the greatest economic question of our era. At the moment, the best guess is it can continue for a few more years. But the economic wheels could just as easily come off. Perhaps even soon.

Even if China does continue to prop up its banks and businesses, it ultimately cannot avoid the issue of its excess capacity. Only the combination of time and a reduction in the rate at which it builds new things can do that. The best case for China is a continued deceleration of growth.

Japan offers guidance: It can be viewed as a Dickensian "ghost of Christmas future" for China and other economies, perhaps all them. Japan is at the very opposite end of the crisis spectrum from China. China is a country on the precipice of a potential crisis. Japan had its crisis in 1991 and is still living in the extended aftermath.

In the 1980s, Japan had rapidly rising private debt and very low central government debt to GDP, just like China today.

In the 1990s, after a rapid rise, Japan's private debt to GDP crested at 221 percent and has been on a slow decline ever since, a decline that exerts considerable deflationary pressure on the country. It still stands at a high level of 168 percent. In 1991, Japan's government debt to GDP stood at only 68 percent. It skyrocketed to 226 percent in the years since, in part because of its recession and in part because of efforts to offset the adverse effects of its private deleveraging. (See Charts 6a and 6b.)

The situation in Japan is cautionary, and with its constant specter of deflation stands as a warning to other major countries. Japan has still not fully recovered from its crisis. It still has high levels of private debt even after significant private debt deleveraging. It is one of the few countries in the developed world where public debt is larger than private debt. Most concerning, in the twenty-three years since the crisis, Japan has seen very low real per capita GDP growth, well less than 1 percent per annum.

I discuss these issues and our proposed policy remedies for both China and Japan further in Chapter 2.

Chapter 2

The Deleveraging Challenge

America reached a major crisis point in the late 1920s and again in the 2000s after periods of rapid private loan growth. However, the economic outcomes after these two crises were very different, a direct consequence of very different policy responses.

Deleveraging in the United States and Japan

In the Great Depression, two major things happened that, along with loan write-offs, caused private loans to drop precipitously, nominally 22 percent or $33 billion in less than four years.

First, a run on the banks in the form of deposit withdrawals forced those banks to call in existing loans and discontinue making new ones. Second, there was a mindset that liquidation—the forced repayment of loans—was the correct remedy for the excesses that had led to the crisis. Secretary of the Treasury Andrew Mellon memorably stated, "Liquidate labor, liquidate stocks, liquidate the farmers, liquidate real estate. It will purge the rottenness out of the system." This all led to an almost unprecedented nominal GDP contraction of 45 percent. Unemployment skyrocketed to 25 percent.

This liquidation mind-set exacerbated GDP contraction because, roughly speaking, a dollar in net paydown of debt results in a dollar or more of GDP reduction since the money that would have been spent on goods and services was instead used to pay down debt. So in less than four years in the early 1930s, a nominal $33 billion or 22 percent reduction in loans helped lead to a $47 billion or 45 percent contraction in GDP. In Chart 12, note how parallel the lines are that indicate the nominal declines in private debt and GDP from the time of the stock market crash until mid-1933. Since the nominal loan contraction in the 2008 crisis was only 2 percent compared to this

Chart 12: The Great Depression, US 1919–1939
Nominal GDP, Federal and Private Debt

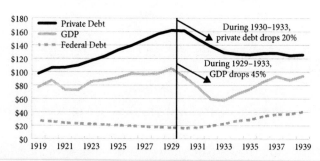

Sources: GDP (1929–1939) data from Bureau of Economic Analysis; all private debt data and GDP (1919–1928) data from Bureau of Economic Analysis, Survey of Current Business, October 1950; federal debt data from treasurydirect.gov.

22 percent, it is hard to conceive today what a colossal reduction that was.

This liquidation mind-set led to the damage of many otherwise healthy businesses and stable households because, for example, even the healthiest businesses suffer if their working capital lines are taken from them.

Just as the growth of private loans is a primary driver of GDP growth, the experience of 1930 to 1933 shows that a reduction in private loans is also a key driver of a reduction in GDP growth.

In the 2008 crisis, there were collapses in the stock and real estate markets and a rise in unemployment to 9.9 percent, but these were modest declines in nominal private loans and GDP as compared to the Great Depression. In the year after the 2008 crisis, a nominal 2.4 percent decline in private loans drove a nominal 2.1 percent annual decline in GDP. (See Chart 13.)

The pain was far less than in the 1930s because major deleveraging was largely avoided. But the fact that major deleveraging was avoided left the United States with higher remaining private debt to GDP.

In 1991, Japan suffered a massive financial crisis, but there was no net paydown in loans—in fact, private loans increased—so initially, there was no nominal contraction of GDP yearly. By the time loans in Japan started to contract in 1995, there was a massive increase in government debt to offset it. This left Japan with extraordinarily high levels of private debt to GDP. The outcome in Japan has been weak growth in GDP for the past twenty-three years.

A large net paydown of debt meant a major contraction of GDP but also left a lower ratio of private debt to

Chart 13: Crisis of 2007–2008, US 1990–2012
Nominal GDP, Private and Federal Debt

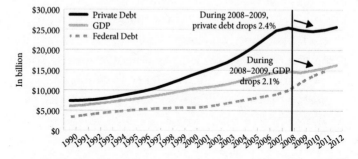

Sources: GDP data from BEA; private debt data from Federal Reserve; federal debt data from treasurydirect.gov.

GDP. Little or no net paydown of private loans meant little or no net reduction of GDP but a higher ratio of leftover private debt to GDP.

Crisis Prevention and Recovery

A government can and should act before lending reaches runaway levels. With a cautionary benchmark of 18 percent growth in five years, regulators should go on high alert as growth approaches this benchmark. At that point, they can intervene preemptively to prevent overcapacity from occurring by reviewing lending policies, increasing capital requirements, and closing loopholes used to circumvent capital requirements. Beyond this, the Federal Reserve could use the pace of private loan growth as a factor in setting interest rates to help counteract rapid loan growth. Rating agencies could give more weight to both the pace of private loan growth and the absolute level of private debt in their ratings of a given country's public debt.

However, these cautionary practices are rarely employed in time. But with the lessons learned from past crises, we know the one primary policy and the one secondary policy (both explained presently) that a government should follow. Our recommended policy formula is similar in many respects to the policies that were employed in the 2008 crisis, but there are important differences. Had this formula been followed by the US government in the 2008 crisis, there would have been a better and faster resolution of the crisis.

The primary policy is to keep lending institutions alive and prudently lending to healthy, deserving borrowers. If net private loans contract, especially if that contraction goes beyond addressing bad loans and begins to impact otherwise healthy borrowers, there is an unnecessary and negative impact on GDP. The secondary policy is to relieve borrowers of unwisely borrowed, crushing debt accumulated during the boom.

If a government intervenes early enough and strongly enough using this primary policy, the adverse effect of the crisis on GDP and unemployment can be significantly mitigated. High debt levels, which do not alone precipitate a crisis but leave a country vulnerable and constrain GDP growth, only get mitigated if government intervenes with this secondary policy.

Unfortunately, both of these policies are controversial, laden with implications of unfairness, wealth transfer, and moral hazard. It's only during a crisis that incurably cautious politicians can be moved to do whatever it takes for fear of being blamed for not having done enough should things get worse.

A crucial point missed in the crisis of 2008 is that government regulators can keep a lending institution operating and lending even if that institution fails—so long as the "failure" is through a government takeover and that institution immediately reopens. In fact, this has been a norm in postwar regulatory history. In more ordinary times, if a bank had made so many bad loans that it became technically insolvent, the regulators would come to that bank on, say, a Friday afternoon, close that bank, fire the CEO and the board of directors, take ownership of the bank (thus wiping out the existing stockholders), and then reopen that bank for business on, say, the following Monday morning.

This approach has a beneficial aspect in that it means the majority of employees keep their jobs and bank borrowers that were otherwise in good condition do not have unnecessary pressure to pay down their loans and thus suffer unnecessary damage to their businesses. It means that counterparties—such as other banks that had loaned money to that bank (as routinely happens)—do not suffer a loss.

In this situation, the government can, in due course, either sell that bank to a competitor or sell its stock in that bank to the public, making government ownership of that bank temporary. A variation on that solution is to let a healthy bank buy an unhealthy one at the moment of failure, using government assistance and indemnifications.

This approach was ignored for most of the largest banks and lenders during the 2008 crisis because they were viewed as too large and complex to be dealt with in this way and, in part, because of their political influence. Large banks that would have failed without government assistance were not allowed to fail. Instead, they were propped up with government assistance and allowed to continue to operate. Their CEOs and boards kept their jobs. This had the beneficial effect of keeping the banks alive and lending, thereby meeting our first policy objective. But it brought with it moral hazard, unfairness, and wealth transfer. The very CEOs and boards that had made the billions of dollars in unwise loans that had led to the crisis got to keep their jobs. Stockholders and bondholders who should have been wiped out were left at least partially intact. Funds and resources that could have been used to write down bad loans and bring relief to borrowers were instead used to rescue stockholders.

On the other end of the spectrum, one large investment banking firm, Lehman Brothers (included in our discussion of banks because, in recent decades, investment banks have become significant lenders), was allowed to fail in a way that meant it also ceased to operate. This meant that counterparties were hurt, employees lost jobs, and there was massive disruption in the market. Had Lehman been taken over as described previously, the damage to the banking system and the economy from the 2008 crisis would have been markedly less.

Our primary policy of keeping lending institutions alive and lending involves two steps: funding and capital. These two steps can happen directly with a government takeover of an institution—a practice I believe should have been employed more in the 2008 crisis—or indirectly by the government providing assistance but stopping short of a takeover.

Funding looks like an obvious step to take. In fact, the primary way banks fail is because they lose their funding, not because they run out of capital. We tend not to think of it this way, but banks are huge borrowers themselves; they don't just make loans, they themselves borrow money in order to fund loans. Banks lose funding because the depositors and lenders that provide them with their funding take their deposits out and don't renew their loans to that bank—causing what we know as a "run" on the bank.

If a bank has enough deposits withdrawn, or if enough of the loans to that bank are not renewed, that bank fails because it has no money to either pay bills or make loans. In fact, banks that are insolvent (i.e., they have a negative net worth) but can still persuade depositors and lenders to put money in their bank can continue to operate if regulators permit.

The government can mitigate or solve this issue by announcing a guarantee to lenders and depositors, by depositing its own money in that bank, or by using its cash to buy loans from that bank.

The second step is to provide capital. If enough of a given bank's loans have gone bad and have been charged off, then that bank's assets (loans are typically a bank's main asset) are less than its liabilities, and it has a negative net worth. The government can solve this problem by buying stock in the bank or by allowing that bank to defer writing off bad loans until some future year—a fiction sometimes enacted for just this purpose and referred to as forbearance. Forbearance is a way of giving the bank time to shore up its capital in other ways—through earnings, a stock sale, or the sale of other assets—before having to write off bad loans. Forbearance can be an explicit policy or an informal, tacit policy.

That brings us to the secondary policy: restructuring loans. This can be a major weapon for the rapid restoration of an economy, but it has been largely underutilized and overlooked. Even if the government takes care of the banks as prescribed previously, there are still a lot of consumers and businesses that have large debts from loans entered into during the boom. Many of these loans were made to buy assets—such as homes or buildings—whose values were artificially inflated because of the boom. So those consumers or businesses are now saddled with loans that are "underwater": The amount owed is now higher than the value of the asset purchased. As mentioned, this high burden of debt has an impact on GDP growth because funds are used to pay interest on this now higher level of debt instead of being spent on goods and services.

A government can provide relief in these situations in two ways. The first is by direct financial assistance to the borrowers: through reimbursement or special tax relief. The cost is born in the current year by the government (and thus the taxpayer) and results in increased government debt. The second way is to simply make the bank take the loss against earnings and thus put them in a place to restructure or forgive debt to the borrower. The problem with this in 2008 was that the amounts were so large that for some banks—and for the system as a whole—taking the loss would have caused them to fail.

I recommend a third way that creates neither a current debt burden for the government nor a current crisis for the banks. The third way is to have banks accelerate the restructuring of debt with borrowers but provide the banks explicit forbearance by allowing them to write off those loans over thirty years and then restructure those debts with borrowers. A similar strategy was employed by regulators in dealing with banks during the Latin American debt crisis of the 1980s and in dealing with the savings and loan crisis in the early 1980s. It does not create a current cost to the government (or taxpayers); it restores purchasing power more quickly to businesses and consumers; and it gives the banks a much longer period of time to deal with the capital and earnings implications of the restructuring. This approach has the important advantage of reducing a country's private debt ratio with little or no increase to its government debt ratio.

Is wealth transfer, moral hazard, or unfairness inherent in this secondary policy? Certainly. But it is inherent in the primary policy as well. You can avoid implementing this secondary policy altogether and thus avoid these difficult issues, but you will be left with consumers and businesses swamped with underwater and unproductive debt.

A government can implement the primary policy at the outset of the crisis. There will be some GDP damage because of the bad debt and overcapacity that has been created. But, as we saw in the United States in 2008 and Japan in 1991, it is likely to be minimal in comparison to the much greater GDP declines that would follow without such action as in the Great Depression.

A government can broadly implement the secondary policy of large-scale debt restructuring almost immediately. This scenario would achieve by far the better result with less leveraged consumers and businesses better positioned to spur GDP growth in the aftermath.

Restoring Growth

Many economists believe government investment programs (often referred to as "stimulus") are the best way to restore growth after a calamity. And this approach works to a degree. However, it has three drawbacks.

First, the private market is generally a better allocator of capital. Second, the enactment of stimulus creates a frenzy of competing special interests and is therefore almost always fraught with spending whose productivity is questionable. Quality of spending matters and is more often than not compromised in these efforts. The third and most notable drawback of stimulus is that it results in higher government debt to GDP.

My recommendation for boosting economic growth is restructuring private debt in lieu of—or perhaps in addition to—government spending. Reducing private debt to GDP through restructuring is a critical but largely neglected way to restore demand, stave off deflation, and stimulate growth. It purges unproductive debt from the system and, paradoxically, it makes room for new and healthier borrowing. Debt growth is a primary driver of income and GDP growth: Lower private debt to GDP means that individuals and businesses have lower debt and therefore more capacity to borrow.

Our work has shown that high levels of private debt increase the vulnerability of economies to calamity, especially at a level in excess of 150 percent to GDP. High private debt also impedes growth, and we find support for this from papers published by International Monetary Fund (IMF) and Bank for International Settlements (BIS) economists. In particular, we look to the work of

Arcand, Berkes, and Panizza in their 2012 paper "Too Much Finance,"[1] which suggests "that finance starts having a negative effect on output growth when credit to the private sector reaches 100% of GDP." This view is supported by the work of Cecchetti, Mohanty, and Zampolli in their 2011 paper "The Real Effects of Debt,"[2] which concludes, "When corporate debt goes beyond 90% of GDP, it becomes a drag on growth. And for household debt, we report a threshold around 85% of GDP, although the impact is very imprecisely estimated."

But how can we reduce private debt to GDP? If high private debt to GDP constrains the level of economic growth and if by reducing it we boost economic growth, what is the best way to do that?

First, let's clarify that I am talking about private debt and not public debt. Public debt to GDP can be reduced in a couple of key ways that private debt cannot. Strong growth in private debt itself is one of the most important things that can bring a reduction in public debt, as was the case in the United States in the 1950s and 1960s. Among other things, it results in short-term boosts to private sector incomes and thus increases government tax receipts.

I know only four methods (short of revolution) that have been advanced as ways to reduce private debt. They are (1) paying down debt, (2) growth, (3) inflation or financial repression, and (4) debt restructuring.

If the means for reducing debt is paying down that debt such that there is a meaningful reduction in aggregate private loans to GDP, GDP will be impacted, as we saw clearly in the Great Depression. That's because money that would have otherwise been spent on goods and services is diverted, and GDP is the measure of aggregate spending. There are essentially no instances of a pain-free deleveraging where it was truly a significant and simultaneous reduction of both public and private debt.

Growth is often touted as the way to reduce government debt, and it can. However, growth can't significantly reduce private debt because growth never occurs over any sustained period unless private debt growth is the same or higher. This is a crucial point. We can't rely on economic growth to reduce the ratio of private debt to GDP more than a very small amount because there are no examples where this has actually happened. Net exports are a form of growth that could allow for an improvement in the private debt ratio. But in the larger countries I am focused on, the amounts of potential net export growth are quite small relative to the size of the private debt problem. Even in the best case, it would take a generation or more to see meaningful improvement from this strategy.

Inflation is often cited as a method for improving the debt ratio, and this concept is somewhat applicable, especially to government debt. But the private debt ratios of many large economies are so high that, again, it would take a generation or more to meaningfully impact the ratios through inflation in the best of circumstances. One variation of this approach that is being employed today is "financial repression": negative real interest rates that are essentially a tax on bondholders and savers. The Fed has pushed down rates hoping to inflate asset prices, especially home values and stock prices. But even with this, the private debt ratio is still 18 percent higher than in 2000, 56 percent higher than in 1980, and almost triple the level of 1950.

So none of these three paths work to any meaningful degree in any reasonable time frame. Ours is a process of elimination that only leaves debt restructuring. We've shown that rising private debt levels have an adverse economic impact and that none of the methods previously described work in a way that significantly reduces private debt to GDP.

So if our already high levels of private debt are a long-term issue, if none of the methods previously described meaningfully reduce that ratio, and if no other methods can be brought forward, then we are left with two options: We can ignore it, which has happened in the past and is likely to happen again, or find ways to restructure debt.

We may recoil from this because of the objections already noted, but it is the only solution that can bring a meaningful near-term reduction to private debt to GDP levels. It engenders objections relating to unfairness, moral hazard, and wealth transfer. There is an objection to the idea based on the view that reducing debt will simply allow borrowers to "repeat the sin." These objections deserve consideration, and we will address them more fully later in this book.

But we must note that restructuring debt with borrowers has *always* been an ordinary and routine activity for lenders. For example, if a business borrower is badly delinquent, a lender will sometimes reduce the principal balance of the loan so that the borrower can successfully make payments.[3]

It's just that in a crisis, so many bad loans have been made and therefore the aggregate amounts are so large that an ordinary restructuring of them all at once would exceed lenders' capital and reserves and cause them to fail. To put it in context, in the early 2000s, the entire US commercial banking industry charged off roughly $30 billion per year. ("Charge-off" is an industry term for when a bad loan is partially or wholly written off as a loss.) But our estimate is that more than $2.5 trillion in problem loans were made from 2001 to 2007, an amount that dwarfed the normal charge-off levels of the industry. The banking system only had $1.5 trillion in capital, so charging off a large portion of them using ordinary practices would have jeopardized the solvency of the industry.

In ordinary times, debt restructuring is routine, so the issues of fairness, moral hazard, and wealth transfer do not draw attention. It is only the massive scale of bad loans made during the crisis, and the resulting massive scale of restructuring needed to deal with it, that brings these issues to the forefront.

How can we go about debt restructuring when the amount to be restructured is so high that it would impair the industry?

First and foremost, I would only advocate a one-time special restructuring. And one-time or short-term programs for dealing with debt restructurings have ample precedent—the bankruptcy laws in England in the early 1700s, the US bankruptcy laws of the 1840s, and the Federal Reserve's method of dealing with the aftermath of the Latin American debt crisis of the 1980s, among many others. These were all intended as short-term programs to deal with the aftermath of a crisis. The very fact that our proposal would be a one-time program would make the issues of moral hazard, fairness, and wealth transfer somewhat easier to deal with.

Second, it should be specifically targeted. We suggest one of the first places to go would be the remaining underwater mortgages: mortgages where the amount is greater than the appraised value of the home. Another would be troubled home equity or second lien mortgages, especially those tied to underwater or troubled first mortgages.

Third, I would recommend doing it in a way that doesn't add to the current federal debt. I don't want the government to take on the full problem in the current year.

Here's how to do it: allow lenders to restructure and spread the loss over thirty years. This type of approach has been used by regulators on a smaller scale in the past. It could be done in part by regulatory fiat: giving the banks a dispensation to write off the loans over an extended period instead of in the current year. A bank could restructure an underwater mortgage with a borrower today, but instead of taking the loss in the current year, that bank would take one-thirtieth of that loss each year. Simple. And to give the banks an incentive, supplement this with not only the normal tax loss benefit but also a modest tax credit recognized over the same period.

Here's a hypothetical framework illustrating how it could work. The government would work with bank regulators, the Financial Accounting Standards Board and the Internal Revenue Service, to enact one-time, limited-duration changes to make all of the following possible:

1. The program would last only twelve to twenty-four months from enactment.
2. The bank would have the option of restructuring with the borrower in the following way: If the mortgage was $300,000 and the appraised value of the home was $200,000, the principal could be reduced to 75 percent (or some other appropriately

conservative percentage) of the current appraised value, or $150,000.

3. If and only if restructured, the loss ($150,000, in our example) would be entered into a deferred loss account for regulatory purposes and written off over thirty years.

4. Each year, the bank would receive the normal tax deduction from the write-off, plus a special tax credit designed to make them whole from an earnings standpoint for that year's loss.

5. Regulators would not include the amount in the deferred loss account for calculating that bank's reserve and capital adequacy.

6. For both generally accepted accounting principles (GAAP) and tax accounting, the loss would be taken in the year of the restructuring, but the present value of tax loss benefits and the additional tax credits could be recognized in the current period in a way that would be designed to fully offset the loss.

7. Since a large number of these loans exist outside of the banking industry, and we want to extend this program to all loans, we would propose that banks be allowed to purchase loans from nonbank holders of loans at a privately negotiated rate and then utilize this program to restructure those loans.

Such a program would have been highly beneficial in 2008. If enacted then, borrowers would be stronger today, and their strength would be reflected in higher current GDP growth. It should be enacted in future crises. It is urgently needed in places like Spain and Portugal today.

During and after the 2008 crisis, banks and other lenders, the US government and the Federal Reserve system acted in concert with other regulators to make sure that a large portion of problem loans were successfully written down. A primary mechanism was the very low interest rates engineered by the Federal Reserve. That had the effect of improving lender operating earnings, and high operating earnings allowed lenders to use those earnings to offset the write-down of those loans over time. Regulators also exercised some degree of informal "forbearance" by giving some banks time to write off loans. Further, in the early days of the crisis, the Federal Reserve purchased large amounts of loans from lenders, which had the effect of freeing up lenders' capital and loss reserves to support the bad debt that remained on their books. Through these and other efforts, I estimate that no more than several hundred billion of these problem loans remain. A large part of these are mortgage loans and home equity loans that are current yet still underwater.

Many of these loans have not been restructured with the borrowers. Therefore, a big potential benefit—freeing up these consumers to increase their spending—has not been fully achieved.

So why our concern, given that the US economy is now progressing? What was wrong with the way the crisis was handled?

I concede that currently the type of restructuring I propose is more needed in Europe than in the United States. But even in the United States, private debt is still too high. Artificially low interest rates have mitigated and masked the impact of this, but these same low rates have harmed savers and created new bubbles. These new bubbles primarily benefit large asset holders—the wealthy—instead of the stressed middle- and lower-income groups. And large-scale lenders have had their imprudence rewarded: The lesson is that if you make too many imprudent loans, even with new laws, the government will rescue you.

How should it have been handled?

We should have provided liquidity support to lenders and guaranteed that those banks would continue operating, even if that required a government takeover.

Some banks should have been allowed to fail, but in the manner described earlier in this book—a manner that would have allowed those banks to continue to operate under government control.

The way to do this would have been as follows: The necessary write-down of loans should have been calculated using conservative practices. If a given lender was still solvent, even if below regulatory minimums (the specific net worth cutoff is open to debate), that lender would have been supported with funding, allowed to continue to operate, and given time to raise supplemental capital. If the write-down resulted in a net worth below that cutoff or a negative net worth, the government would then have taken over that institution, the CEO and board would have been replaced, and shareholders and bondholders would have lost their investment. However, since the institution would have kept operating according to long-standing regulatory policies for takeovers, few if any counterparties or otherwise healthy borrowers would have been affected.

Lenders not taken over by the government could have written off certain bad loans over an extended period using the program described previously. As part of this, loans would have been restructured with borrowers. This restructuring would have enabled those borrowers to have been more vigorous participants in the economy and better positioned them to have contributed to the recovery.

If the recommendations I outline here had been implemented, the result would have been far fewer underwater mortgages, fewer constraints to buying and selling, and a housing market more rapidly returned to healthy pricing and sales activity levels. Crucially, moral hazard for lenders would have been avoided, since it was lenders' loose policies that were the true culprit in the crisis. Fewer small businesses and individuals would have been hurt, and impaired banks would have been repaired and restored to appropriate operating levels more quickly and been better positioned to continue to supply credit. The Federal Reserve would still have lowered interest rates, but it would not have needed to reduce them as dramatically; therefore, small savers would not have been as adversely impacted, and new bubbles would not have been as readily created. Markets would have normalized more quickly. Real estate markets in particular would not now be as dependent on ultralow interest rates. Consumer demand would be stronger today because fewer consumers would be overburdened with the unreasonable debt levels reached in the precrisis period. Private debt levels would now be lower, and GDP, unemployment, and government debt levels would be better. In short, we would be better off today.

The suggestion of the type of debt restructuring proposed here brings the fear that if you let borrowers off the hook this time, they will be incented to misbehave again. There are, however, certain things to consider when assessing the unfairness, wealth transfer, and moral hazard implications of restructuring.

First of all, in the process of saving financial institutions during the 2008 crisis, such concerns were set aside in any case, and policies with enormous unfairness, wealth transfer, and moral hazard implications were enacted. But the benefits flowed to lenders and their shareholders rather than to borrowers.

Of course, two wrongs don't make a right. And if our nation's policies violated principles of fairness, wealth transfer, and moral hazard to the benefit of these lenders, that does not necessarily make it right to help borrowers. But benefiting those borrowers in need of relief benefits the entire economy.

There are steps that can be taken to mitigate legitimate objections to restructuring, such as making programs one-time-only and income qualified.

And even with a one-time program, borrowers don't get off unscathed: The default is on their credit record, their credit bureaus, and other industry reports and will likely affect future loan decisions regarding those individuals and businesses. This may well cause future loan requests to be declined, priced at a higher rate, and subject to more stringent terms.

I will make a policy recommendation in the last chapter of this book—namely, higher capital requirements for lenders—that I believe will mitigate the possibility of runaway lending and reorient economic growth toward less financing-dependent growth.

A person's morality is not likely to be changed by a one-time restructuring dispensation. Further, it took years to get to this point, so pursuant to a one-time restructuring program, we would hardly get there again overnight, especially if the capital requirement reforms I propose are adopted.

Recommendations for China and Beyond

In China, very high lending growth, most of which has been to businesses, has already created major issues. China's ghost cities already attest to this. And its decline in GDP growth from 14 percent GDP growth to 7.8 percent in five years underscores the point.

The time for China's government to act is now, which may already be happening. China currently appears to be cautiously approaching this subject—even though it has the capacity to keep the lending-growth-fueled party going for some time.

I estimate that the level of problem loans in China is no less than 10 percent of GDP, or roughly $1 trillion, and could be as high as 30 percent of GDP, or roughly $3 trillion.

China's government has ample capacity to deal with this problem if it moves forward appropriately. It holds financial assets roughly equal to 35 percent of GDP. Its central government borrowings are only 32 percent of GDP—as compared to 100 percent for the United States and 226 percent for Japan—so presumably, it has more than enough capacity to borrow to the level of an additional 30 percent of GDP or more. Because of this, it can recapitalize lenders using its existing financial resources and does not need to use the thirty-year forbearance approach recommended for Europe and the United States earlier in this book.

But China risks a crisis if it does not act. For China, the appropriate path forward will involve recapitalizing banks in an amount sufficient to offset the write-down of bad loans, causing those banks to restructure loans to certain borrowers, and extending employment programs and the social safety net to mitigate any resulting household employment or income challenges as GDP growth slows. In total, the cost of such efforts could total anywhere from 20 percent to 40 percent of GDP.

I believe China should take these initiatives preemptively, and China's government may well be taking tentative steps in this direction now. If so, I applaud them.

But what China cannot easily solve is the problem of the overcapacity they have already created. It will take years for genuine demand to catch up with existing capacity in areas like housing. By engineering the economy to continue to grow at 7 percent per annum (if, in fact, those numbers are reliable), the Chinese government is compounding the problem. GDP growth is a measure of the capacity being created, not a measure of the capacity needed or the capacity actually being absorbed.

To the extent that this 7 percent growth[4] is occurring through the continued increase in loans—and much of it surely is—China and its banks are only adding to the size of the loan problems the government will eventually need to address through its own financial assets and borrowing capacity. China should instead target lower GDP growth levels more commensurate with true growth in demand.

The world has come to depend on the demand resulting from China's frenetic capacity-building. As China recognizes its overcapacity and slows that down, the world—especially its regional neighbors—will feel it. And if China does not act soon to recapitalize its banks and thus lets a banking crisis develop, its suffering will be compounded, and foreign banks that have lent to concerns in China will also take a hit. The ripple effect could be large.

With China's financial capacity, its government can avoid an outright crisis. The outcome could instead simply be a period in which GDP growth slows markedly and China experiences a long period of very low growth while they absorb the significant excess capacity they have now created.

A government's capacity for additional borrowing is one measure of its wealth. If a country is of the size and strength for its government to borrow in times of adversity, that government's additional capacity to borrow is also a measure of its capacity to deal with a crisis. Its borrowing capacity represents reserves that can be utilized to intervene.

Growth in government debt as opposed to private debt is not a primary cause of crises. But that does not mean that high government debt levels don't matter. (By true government debt, I exclude government debt that is employed in a role that private debt ordinarily fills—for example, building factories—as is true in many less developed countries.)

And government debt has increased markedly in many large countries as a direct result of the Great Recession, in part because of the drop-off in tax income revenues as earnings fell because of the recession and in part because of government stimulus and rescue expenditures.

Japan's public debt to GDP was 67.5 percent when it suffered the 1991 crisis and is now 226 percent, going from a moderate level of public debt to among the highest in the developed world in a single generation. The United States is at roughly 100 percent. At 32 percent, China has the least of the three, although both Japan and China hold significant financial assets that make their effective government debt levels far lower than the numbers reported here.

Japan has still-high private debt levels, very high levels of public debt, and a decades-long struggle with deflation and low GDP growth. If rates rise or confidence in their ability to service this public debt ever changes, there well could be issues.

But their first need is to continue to reduce private debt to GDP, preferably more through the kind of restructuring program described in this book rather than relying solely on a continued paydown. This type of restructuring should have been done all at once in the period immediately following its crisis rather than through the slow, GDP-sapping business deleveraging that has actually occurred and has not yet sustainably reversed itself.

In some respects, Japan's struggle with deflation is tied to this. Loan growth can add to demand and firm up prices. The absence of loan growth can soften prices. Japan's deflation is tied in part to its weak or negative private debt to GDP growth. That means restructuring can be part of the solution to deflation by contributing to renewed loan growth.[5]

In Europe, some countries such as Spain and Portugal have an acute need for the type of private debt restructuring prescribed in this book. High levels of private debt, much more than public debt, are the primary impediment to restored vibrancy.

The United States, on a relative basis, finds itself in a better position than most if not all developed countries.

Though its private debt to GDP growth is flat, the United States still has concerning overall levels of private debt to GDP. Like the other countries, it could benefit from selective restructuring programs.

The ideal economic situation for a given country and the world is to have less capacity (or supply) than demand coupled with low private debt. Instead, we have nearly the opposite situation. In the first decade of the 2000s, the United States and Europe built far too much capacity, especially in housing, and incurred too much private debt. In the 1980s, Japan built far too much capacity, saddling its banks with too much private debt and too many bad loans. While all have been catching up to this capacity, none yet has less capacity than demand, and all still have high private debt. And now China, whose industrialization and urbanization long fueled global growth, has created its own overcapacity and private debt problem, building far too much capacity in many industrial and real estate projects with easy credit that fueled the most rapid buildup of private debt yet. So now the majority of the globe is in this less than desirable place. No major global economic player now has that pivotal combination of undercapacity and low private debt to fuel productive investment and help boost global growth.[6]

Much has been written of late regarding the decline of the middle class. It is important to note that the size of the middle class grows in major countries (or the world) when there is too little capacity and low private debt (like after World War II). That is because a middle class is needed to build new capacity. Corporate debt can be used to fund the *building* of new capacity while consumer debt can be used to fund the *consumption* of that capacity. In contrast, the size of the middle class plateaus or shrinks when there is too much capacity and too much debt (like there is at the present). Stated differently, inequality increases when there is high capacity and high debt; it decreases when capacity and debt are low.

Chapter 3

The Long-Term View

In 1950, the level of private debt in the United States was 55 percent to GDP. Today, it is 156 percent. Our investigation has led us to conclude that the level of private debt alone is not predictive of a crisis—it takes rapid private debt growth as well.

But high private debt, which is often the residue in the aftermath of runaway debt growth, makes an economy more susceptible to future crisis and impedes growth.

The more debt businesses and consumers have, the more vulnerable they are to economic distress because of the interest on that debt and their repayment obligations. And the more debt they have, the less capacity they have to borrow additional funds to sustain themselves through adverse circumstances.

Some maintain that the net impact of increased private debt is neutral, since for every borrower, there is a lender. But since wealth is highly concentrated, the burden of increased debt falls disproportionately on the middle- and lower-income groups—the very consumers we rely on to power broad economic growth. Higher debt levels and interest expenses have a much more immediate impact on reducing business and household spending than they do on increasing the spending and consumption of lenders. And to the extent that some portion of this is only a timing difference, these timing differences have an ongoing rather than one-time impact when debt is continually rising.

Some point to the fact that the consumer debt service ratio has returned to precrisis levels. But this is false comfort since it is largely a function of artificially low current interest rates.

A country's overall GDP growth tends to decline as it gets larger, and there are many factors—decelerating population growth among them—that can influence that growth. Among those factors are higher business and consumer debt.

Some would argue that business debt produces income in excess of the debt. However, business debt is being created faster than business income (see Chart 14). Businesses are becoming more leveraged.

Some analysts minimize the concern about rising business debt, saying that a significant portion is incurred to buy back stock. But buybacks are small relative to the total business loans outstanding, and in aggregate, the buyback number doesn't have much impact on the long-term trends. Similarly, the amount of debt incurred because business cash is kept overseas for tax reasons is small relative to the whole.

With regard to consumer debt, 70 percent or more of all consumer debt is mortgage debt, so a closer look at mortgage debt is in order.

If mortgage debt is simply displacing rent payments, it does not reduce individual consumption. But the

Chart 14: Business Debt to Business Income

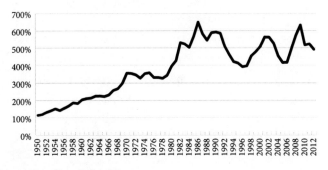

Source: Data from Federal Reserve.

evidence suggests that consumers stretch to buy homes that are significantly larger than if they had remained renters, and thus mortgage debt does in fact impact other forms of household consumption.

Mortgages are viewed as good for consumers because they allow those consumers to build wealth in a way that renting would not allow and are seen as promoting a culture of ownership and responsibility.

Home ownership through mortgages has been a good investment but primarily because of the massive tax advantages. It is good but not as good as widely believed. In fact, it was too much of this good thing—runaway home buying encouraged by profligate lenders—that contributed mightily to the 2008 crisis.

Here I would make a few observations: Since 1946, in inflation adjusted dollars, US mortgage debt per person has increased by $28,000, and the result has been a net increase in home value (home value minus mortgage value) of $21,400. In other words, for all the focus on the mortgage market over 60+ years, consumers have incurred $28,000 more in debt to get an additional per capita $21,400 in net worth. We estimate that even with the massive tax advantages afforded to mortgages, consumers would have been as well off if they had taken the down payment, put it in stocks, and rented instead. Some commentators, such as Yale economist Robert Shiller, go further by saying that home ownership is overrated as an investment, explaining that "it takes maintenance, it depreciates, it goes out of style."[7]

Net home value (home value minus mortgage amount) is only 14 percent of per capita net worth. In 2012, the net home value per person was $33,000. Luckily, the consumer has many other assets—deposits, investments, pensions—for a total per capita net worth of $225,739.

And the ratio of US consumer net worth to income—excluding pensions—has actually declined during the period in which the rate of home ownership has increased.

Countries such as Germany and Switzerland, like the United States in emphasizing values of probity and civic responsibility, have a much lower percentage of home ownership. As noted by Richard Florida and Charlotta Mellander in a study of forty-two leading nations,[8] less-developed countries generally have higher levels of home ownership than more developed ones. The United States aside, home ownership most often declines as nations get wealthier.

The Bigger Picture: Our Future Debt Challenge

The modern economic era started around 1800, fresh on the heels of the Industrial Revolution, bringing dramatic change as you can see in Chart 15.

Chart 15: World Average GDP per Capita

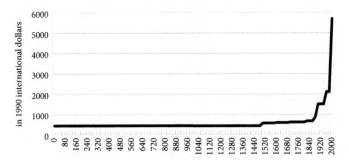

Source: J. Bolt and J. L. van Zanden, "The First Update of the Maddison Project: Re-Estimating Growth Before 1820" (working paper 4, Maddison Project, 2013).

It has been a remarkable era, and untold benefits have been realized: improved mortality rates, the creation of a global middle class, increased leisure time, and much more. Most of the things we equate with broad prosperity have arisen during this era.

But there has been a relatively unnoticed dimension to this era. Over the course of this entire period, the growth in debt has meaningfully exceeded the growth in GDP. And within that long expanse, GDP growth has never exceeded debt growth for more than a few consecutive years.

One reason rapid lending growth is possible is that financial institutions have enjoyed the ability to operate at very high levels of leverage. In today's world, that is typically ten to one, or more. And the trend toward placing loans with individuals and less-regulated institutions will only increase the trend toward increased leverage, because it further eliminates the need for capital in order to lend.

This phenomenon is so evident that it is possible to conclude that debt growth in excess of GDP—especially private debt growth in excess of GDP—is a necessary part of GDP growth. There have been no extended periods in the last two hundred years where debt growth has not exceeded GDP growth (see Chart 16), and the most notable periods in which GDP growth exceeded debt growth were in the calamitous aftermath of the crash of 1929 and to a lesser extent, the aftermath of World War II.

In Charts 17 and 18, note further that the three biggest panics of the 1800s—the panics of 1837, 1873, and 1893—have a pattern of massive, rapid credit buildup followed by a decline in credit that conforms to our thesis. And yet,

Chart 16: Total Debt to GDP 1866–2012, Bank and Federal Debt
Only 1819–1865, Federal Debt Only 1790–1818

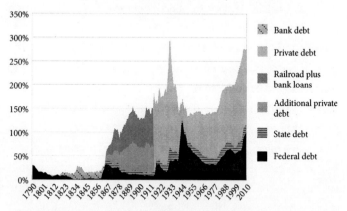

Sources: Bank debt-1816-1865- US Census; Private debt 1866-1915- actual railroad bonds from Poor's Manual of Railroads, plus Bank loans from US Census, plus additional private debt from author's calculations based on Goldsmith's Comparative National Balance Sheets; Private debt 1916-1944- BEA; 1945-2012- Federal Reserve; State debt- 1866-1915- Author's Calculations based on Goldsmith, 1916-1944- BEA; 1945-2012- Federal Reserve; Federal debt 1790-2012- Treasurydirect.gov

as is often the case, in referring to the Panic of 1837, an author recently repeated the familiar refrain that "no one knows the cause."

But we do know.

Private debt to GDP growth is now relatively flat after the modest post-2008 deleveraging. All major categories of private debt are now ascending except household mortgages, which still suffer in the aftermath of the 2008 crisis because of the lack of restructuring. And, of course, public debt levels have exploded because of the crisis.

Perhaps the phenomenon of debt growth exceeding GDP growth will someday end. Perhaps the higher private debt levels get, the harder it is for those debt levels to grow further. Higher debt levels on the part of borrowers make lenders less inclined to lend more, and more money spent to service debt is a drag on growth, which has at least some curbing effect on the need for debt.

Perhaps the hypergrowth in GDP per capita of the last two centuries was possible only because it began

Chart 17: Panic of 1837, Bank Loans to GDP

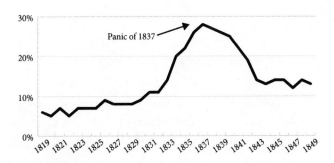

Sources: GDP data from CBO; bank loans data from *Historical Statistics of the United States, Colonial Times* to 1970.

Chart 18: Panics of 1873 and 1893, Railroad Debt to GDP

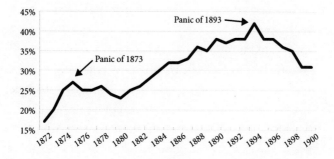

Sources: GDP data from CBO; railroad debt data from *Historical Statistics of the United States, Colonial Times to 1970* and *Poor's Manual of Railroads*.

with low leverage, and now that the globe has a much higher level of leverage, GDP is inherently constrained and lower long-term growth is inevitable. Or, just as likely and certainly healthier, perhaps constraints on debt that result from high overall debt levels will bias future growth away from financing-dependent types of growth. It may be that the high level of leverage with which lenders have been allowed to operate has skewed GDP growth toward financing-dependent forms of growth, and if lenders were required to operate with lower levels of leverage, that bias would change to less-financing dependent forms.

In any event, rapid GDP growth over a decade or more has virtually always been accompanied by correspondingly high debt growth (or extraordinary periods of high net exports), and if debt growth once again becomes high, we will once again be sailing between Scylla and Charybdis.

A Reform Agenda

We should want loan growth, just loan growth that is more moderate and remains below the rough thresholds discussed in this book. We've often had far too much of a good thing.

As noted previously, some critics have suggested that even if we enact the kind of large-scale, one-time debt restructuring programs advocated in this book to remediate the economy after a crisis, private debt to GDP will inevitably rise again to current levels. There is some truth to this as we have seen: Rising debt to GDP levels are the story of the past two hundred years.

However, we can moderate the level of loan growth in excess of GDP by modifying laws and regulations in two critical areas: capital requirements and restructuring laws.

These are two straightforward policies that can both slow the ascent of the private debt to GDP ratio and reduce the probability of runaway lending. They are (1) increasing the effective capital requirements for lending institutions (including closing capital requirement loopholes) and (2) shifting the balance of restructuring and bankruptcy law in the favor of the borrower.

Banks and other lenders have capital requirements they must meet in order to lend money. For banks, these requirements—and not deposit availability or reserve requirements—are the primary constraints on their and the system's ability to make more loans.

One of the reasons that rapid lending growth is possible is that financial institutions have been able to operate at very high levels of leverage.

To oversimplify, banks today generally have to meet roughly a 10 percent capital requirement. If a bank wants to make a billion dollars in loans and the capital requirement is 10 percent, then it needs to raise $100 million in capital to make the loans. If the capital requirement is 15 percent, then it needs to raise $150 million in capital to make the loans. It's obviously harder to raise $150 million than $100 million. And having a higher capital requirement— all other things being equal—reduces shareholder returns, thus potentially making a bank a less attractive investment (though if they were made higher for all lenders, industry economics would adjust to restore that attractiveness). So it's no surprise then that lenders are always seeking ways to reduce their capital requirements.

In the past, this has been done in a variety of ways, including through such techniques as asset securitization— which allows a lender to "sell" the loans but continue to receive almost all the earnings from them. Another method has been for banks to use the latitude regulators give them to ascribe less risk to certain loans and thus carry less capital to support them. Banks continually seek new ways such as these to minimize required capital.

Generally, while lower capital requirements mean that a bank can raise less capital, or make more loans with the same capital, it also means the bank has less strength when trouble comes. And what is true for a single bank is also true for the system as a whole.

Runaway credit periods have often been fueled in part as bankers have learned to circumvent capital requirements or have operated in areas where appropriate capital requirements were not in place. Regulators rightly attempt to know all the nuances of such exotic instruments (e.g., credit default swaps, securitizations, and shadow banking) to be able to assess whether capital requirements have been circumvented.

But there is a more straightforward way to assess whether capital requirements are being circumvented and are thus spurring runaway lending growth: simply keeping track of total private loans—regardless of the type of lender or loan. If they begin to approach roughly 18 percent to GDP in five years, it's time to worry. We don't have to get inside lenders' secret chambers; we can use this top-down gauge to assess whether too many problem loans are being made.

Higher capital requirements—especially those which properly recognize and require appropriate capital for "off-balance sheet" instruments, insurance contracts, and other structures yet to be devised that have the purpose of circumventing capital requirements—will be a check on runaway lending and will bias the economy toward ways to grow that are less dependent on financing. This will make the financial sector less crisis prone and create more sustainable growth.

The top-down gauge would allow us to get at the problem. Part of the solution is increasing capital requirements beyond those being implemented today. The new capital requirements being implemented as of this writing are estimated to require US banks to add less than $100 billion in new capital—a low number compared to the $2 trillion of problem loans generated in the last crisis.

Another policy change that would mitigate runaway lending would be a shift toward more borrower-friendly restructuring laws. At present, the laws are neither fish nor fowl but fall somewhere in the middle. Those laws could be rewritten to completely favor the lender or the borrower. I advocate neither extreme. In the broad middle, however, it is still possible to shade the laws somewhat in favor of either the lender or the borrower. This brings me to another paradox in banking: In my experience as a lender, the more in favor of the borrower the law is, the more prudent the lender will be, because that lender will know that in the event of a default, it will have a less favorable legal position. That very fact concentrates the mind—this time, in favor of prudence.

As evidence of this, look at the Bankruptcy Reform Act of 2005 that made it more difficult for borrowers to file for Chapter 7 bankruptcy. This emboldened lenders and led to easier credit at the very moment when prudence would have been the better course. Ironically, it likely brought very little, if any, reduction in loss levels.

The policy changes recommended here would have the effect of influencing growth toward channels that are more dependent on true inventions and productivity breakthroughs and less dependent on financing—a growth that is more durable and much less likely to end in a financial meltdown.

These two steps would bring us very close to a solution to our two-hundred-year-old dilemma and usher us across the threshold to a new era of more sustainable economic growth.

Conclusion

Private lending growth, unchecked, has repeatedly caused crises. When it comes to the matter of lending, the invisible hand, as valuable as it otherwise is, needs a restraining hand.

For the larger countries of the world, no other criteria are remotely as effective in explaining or predicting financial crises as the combined criteria of very rapid private loan growth and high overall private loans to GDP. That indicator is the flashing light that should alarm every finance minister and concerned citizen in the world. And the high private debt levels that are the aftermath of runaway lending are then a drag on growth.

In some respects, the thesis of this book is simplicity itself. Financial (or banking) crises come from too many bad loans. And the surest evidence of bad loans is runaway loan growth. What looks like success is actually the seeds of failure.

We now have the tools to see that runaway lending growth for what it is: a precursor of crisis at certain levels. We can predict a crisis in major world economies where both the damage internally and the risk of contagion are high. We have tools to prevent these crises from happening and reduce private debt levels that are excessive.

Conclusion

The study of private debt must become a more central part of economic analysis and both rating agency and regulatory review.

I only have one final thought: It's been true from the earliest days of human history until now, from Egypt and Babylon to Israel, that an unsustainable rise in private debt can bring calamity.

But if the past shows us the problem, it may also show us the solution. In biblical Israel, they had a special name for the day when debts were forgiven: Jubilee.

These civilizations have something to teach us: When private debt rises to unsustainable levels, we could do worse than turn to these ancient models of forbearance.

It is private debt that matters most.

Acknowledgments

Writing this book has been a joy and an education. However, as much as this subject has consumed my attention over the past few years, the idea and the credit for my writing the book belong to my editor, Damon Linker, and the University of Pennsylvania Press director, Eric Halpern. I owe them much.

My interest in this subject came from my banking background, but my true enabler was the inimitable Steve Clemons, both in the work we did together and in the introductions he provided me, especially through his marvelous economics conferences. The invaluable, steady hand that guided me on technical issues and kept me from falling too far into the ideological abyss was Sherle Schwenninger, along with his terrific colleagues Josh Freedman, Sam Sherraden, and Ben Kolansky. Ben Yuhas, a highly skilled data modeler and colleague of mine from my banking days, provided critical analytical support. Dan McShane was the true constant throughout the process, mastering the material, providing daily analytical support, and sifting through the fragmented, irregular, and sometimes contradictory data that seem to characterize the world of economics.

Acknowledgments

We conferred with countless economists along the way, but it was a noneconomist, Larry Platt, whose sound judgment and common sense kept things in perspective for me. At a critical juncture, the brilliant Ambassador Joseph Torsella devoted considerable energy into tightening the book's structure and arguments.

However, in the end, it was the magical Margaret Carlson who brightened the entire project and rescued me from the worst of my stilted prose.

We combed through endless data in writing this book and in that regard, want to give our thanks for the generous help and tremendous resources of the Federal Reserve, the Federal Reserve Bank of St. Louis, the Bureau of Economic Analysis, the International Monetary Fund, the Bank for International Settlement, and the United Nations Statistics Division. The United States in particular has enviable economic data collection and presentation practices that the rest of the world would be wise to more closely emulate.

I'd also like to thank the many writers whose work inspired and informed mine, including David Graeber, Yves Smith, Richard Koo, Robert Shiller, Carmen Reinhart, Kenneth Rogoff, Paul McCulley, Alan Taylor, Moritz Schularick, Liaquat Ahamed, Alasdair Roberts, Irving Fisher, Hyman Minsky, Charles Kindleberger, Michael Hudson, Steven Keen, Felix Martin, Michael Lind, Robert Hockett, and others too numerous to mention. Karl Snow and Saurav Karki of Bates White provided important early support, as did the team at Moody's Analytics. Another wonderful economist who provided significant help was Lacy Hunt, to whom I was introduced by my longtime friend and fellow economics enthusiast Rick Reed. Ariel Ron and Brenna O'Rourke helped guide me through the murky depths of nineteenth-century data. My business colleagues Kevin Kleinschmidt and Scott Tarte provided insight and feedback along the way, as did Joe Camarda, Peter Burns, and Ben Craig. I also benefited from the comments on an early draft of the manuscript by Dean Baker, Joerg Bibow, Steve Blitz, Joseph Gagnon, Roger Kubarych, Cary Leahy, and Thomas Palley, who, while often not in agreement with me, nevertheless provided feedback that resulted in substantial improvements to the work. I am truly in their debt.

The credit for any good things you find in this book belong to them, and all the faults are mine alone.

Of course, none of this would have been bearable if I were not surrounded by the friends and family that make my life so rich and full. My Philadelphia Young Presidents' Organization (YPO) forum brothers are always a wonderful sounding board and source of support. My Philadelphia family—my children Lauren, Eric, Davis, and my sister Joanna—are a constant comfort. Thanks are due to my mom and dad, who gave me the gift of curiosity and independent thinking, and to my loving brother Steven. And I also give thanks to my older brother David, whom I have always idolized and who gave me the gift of unbounded confidence. I collaborated with him on my first foray into the world of economics way back when William Miller was chairman of the Federal Reserve and the OPEC minister Sheik Ahmed Zaki Yamani seemed—to us at least—to dominate the world. How could we have known back then how wrong almost everything we were taught would turn out to be?

And last, I extend a special, heartfelt thanks both to my dearest friend, confidante, and co-conspirator, Audrey Taichman, and to my eternal muse and inspiration, Dr. Laura Windham.

Notes

Chapter 1

1. Throughout this book, when we use the term *crisis*, we are referring to a systemic banking crisis as described in a 2012 IMF WP/12/163 authored by Luc Laeven and Fabian Valencia. A systemic crisis is when there are significant signs of financial distress in the banking system as indicated by significant bank runs, losses in the banking system, and/or bank liquidations and significant banking policy intervention measures in response to significant losses in the banking system—including at least three of the following six: extensive liquidity support (5 percent of deposits and liabilities to nonresidents), bank restructuring gross costs (at least 3 percent of GDP), significant bank nationalizations, significant guarantees put in place, significant asset purchases (at least 5 percent of GDP), and deposit freezes and/or bank holidays. (See Appendix H.)

2. We will refer to this as the 2008 crisis from this point forward.

3. Alan Greenspan, *The Map and the Territory: Risk, Human Nature, and the Future of Forecasting* (New York: Penguin Press, 2013), 69.

4. As an aside, after a crisis, people often compare current asset prices to prices that existed at the precrisis peak to assess whether things have fully recovered. However, since those peak values were artificially high, it is often more useful to compare to preboom trends extrapolated to the present.

Notes

5. This means two simple charts—one on top of the other—that together portray that country's debt through time. We call this the "debt snapshot." When focusing on a specific calamity such as the 2008 crisis, we will show a chart covering the years before and after the beginning of that crisis. We show the years prior to the crisis extending from a period when debt growth was relatively flat. So for the 2008 crisis, we include the 1990 to 1997 period when private debt growth was essentially flat. Chart 4a shows the nominal totals for GDP, private debt, and public debt, along with a black vertical line marking the crisis year. The Chart 4b shows private debt and public debt in ratio to GDP with a black dot marking the crisis year. Since the percentage growth in private debt to GDP of 18 percent or more in a five-year span is the key trigger for a crisis, we will include a black-dotted arrow over any five-year period that is close to or above this 18 percent threshold. Of course, a debt snapshot is not a complete picture, but it does provide an orientation. Although we study inflation-adjusted amounts (sometimes referred to as "real") in our analyses, in the debt snapshot, we use actual (sometimes referred to as "nominal") totals as our first level of analysis because "real" often masks part of the story. For example, in the 1930s, looking at the "real" loan decline before looking at the "nominal" decline masks the steepness of this decline. The real decline is less steep because costs were declining—but the decline in prices was in some respects caused by that decline in loans and is thus in part circular, so it is important to start with the nominal. (We include the real charts in Appendix I.) We consider financial debt a very important part of the story, but financial debt growth is a function of the growth in business and household debt—it is often the other side of the balance sheet. And we found that growth in financial debt was not a better predictor of risk than business plus household debt. When it comes to these debt snapshots, we include only government, business, and household debt, because to add in financial institution debt double counts certain debt that would get eliminated in an actual accounting consolidation. So, for example, we calculate the current total debt of the United States as 256 percent—business debt plus household debt plus government debt—instead of 342 percent—business debt plus household debt plus government debt plus financial institution debt.

Notes

Chapter 2

1. Jean-Louis Arcand, Enrico Berkes, and Ugo Panizza, "Too Much Finance?" (working paper, 2012).

2. Stephen G. Cecchetti, M. S. Mohanty, and Fabrizio Zampolli, "The Real Effects of Debt" (working paper, 2011).

3. Usually, this is because the lender recognizes that it will not be fully repaid and calculates that more will get repaid if he or she restructures the loan by forgiving some principal than would be repaid if the borrower continued to try to make payments on the full loan. The lender may determine that if the borrower tried to make payments on the full loan, that borrower might neglect spending the money needed on his or her business operations to insure that the business remains healthy enough to continue to make meaningful loan payments. That's just one of numerous examples of why and how lenders routinely restructure debt.

4. Some have suggested that this 7 percent growth rate is intentionally overstated, and to the extent that it is, less overcapacity is being created.

5. Japan has a deflation problem that is even more fundamental than no loan growth. That problem is its declining population. Inflation fundamentally comes from demand exceeding supply, and loan growth is one source of demand. But population growth is an even more fundamental source of demand.

6. Some of the undercapacity in the mid-twentieth century was a result of accelerating population growth, but population growth is decelerating today.

7. Sam Ro, "Robert Shiller Destroys the Idea of Investing in a Home," *Business Insider* (February 7, 2013), http://www.businessinsider.com/robert-shiller-home-investment-a-fad-2013-2.

8. Richard Florida, "Why the U.S. Needs to Fall out of Love with Homeownership," *The Atlantic* Citylab (September 17, 2013), http://www.theatlanticcities.com/housing/2013/09/why-us-needs-fall-out-love-homeownership/6517.

CPSIA information can be obtained at www.ICGtesting.com
Printed in the USA
LVOW06*1425090714

393587LV00002B/4/P